Computers which can use

CREATING ADVENTURE GAMES ON YOUR COMPUTER

Apple II and IIe
(and compatibles)

Atari

Coleco ADAM

Commodore 64

IBM PC (and compatibles)

Texas Instruments TI 99/4a
(with Extended BASIC)

TRS-80 Models 1, 2, 3, and 100

TRS-80 Color Computer

VIC 20

Plus any computer furnished with Microsoft BASIC
(BASIC conversion instructions included)

Memory requirements: at least 24K RAM

Other books by Tim Hartnell
published by Ballantine Books

TIM HARTNELL'S GIANT BOOK OF COMPUTER GAMES

HOW TO PROGRAM YOUR IBM PC

HOW TO PROGRAM YOUR APPLE IIe

HOW TO PROGRAM YOUR COMMODORE 64

Creating Adventure Games on Your Computer

Tim Hartnell

Ballantine Books • New York

Copyright © 1983, 1984 by Tim Hartnell

All rights reserved under International and Pan-American Copyright Conventions. Published in the United States by Ballantine Books, a division of Random House, Inc., New York, and simultaneously in Canada by Random House of Canada Limited, Toronto.

Certain hardware and software products are mentioned by their trade names in this book. In most—if not all—cases these designations are claimed as trademarks by the respective companies. It is not our intent to use any of these names generically and the reader is cautioned to investigate all claimed trademark rights before using any of these names for any purpose other than to refer to the product described.

Library of Congress Catalog Card Number: 84-90827

ISBN 0-345-31883-8

Designed by Gene Siegel

Cover illustration by Darrell K. Sweet

Cover design by Andrew Newman

Manufactured in the United States of America

First American Edition: August 1984

10 9 8 7 6 5 4 3 2

Contents

APPENDICES

FOREWORD

Why would intelligent people, with access to massive amounts of computer power which could be doing something useful, want to bring their brainpower to bear on the problems of creating and exploring mythical landscapes? Why, when your computer could be earning its keep balancing your checking account, are you forcing it to control a game in which you battle fierce monsters in labyrinthine caverns, envoke magic spells, and uncover vast hordes of Elven gold?

The answer is obvious. Using your computer for serious things all the time is just plain boring. Trekking across alien landscapes, chopping up people with broadswords and axes, haggling with quasi-humanoid creatures in off-world taverns, seems to many people a much better way to spend their time and their computer power.

If you want to add this kind of excitement to your computer, this book is for you.

Adventure games—with or without a computer—have not been with us for long. It was just over a decade ago, in 1974, when the fantasy game *Dungeons and Dragons* was released. D & D (as it quickly became known) triggered an explosion of interest in role-playing games.

Fantasy games grew out of war games, which began life in the final years of the 18th Century as training exercises for real-life army commanders. After the First World War, many people took to playing war games as a hobby, reenacting famous battles and rewriting history as they played.

People all over the States were playing war games, forming into clubs which came together only to do battle. In Lake Geneva, Wisconsin, a war gaming club made a slight departure from the norm, and started an explosion which is still reverberating around the world.

A team from this club, under Gary Gygax, devised a set of war game rules which set the clashes in a mythological, medieval setting where magic worked, dragons flew, and treasure in abundance lay around waiting to be claimed. The rules were published as *Chainmail*.

This was the first part of the mixture which brought fantasy gaming to critical mass. The second part was provided by Dave Arneson in Minneapolis–St. Paul, Minnesota, who decided to set his battles in an underground dungeon. He used the *Chainmail* rules to manage the clashes his players had with wizards, warlocks and the rest. Dave and Gary, it appears, then got together to create a dungeon/game-playing scenario called *Greyhawk*. They codified the rules, and put them together in a little book, and tried to have it published.

None of the established game companies were interested, so in 1974 Gygax formed a company—Tactical Studies Rules (TSR)—to publish the rules himself, under the name *Dungeons and Dragons*. The first printing sold out in less than 12 months.

Dungeons and Dragons fed a widespread hunger which had been primed by the success, in the previous decade, of such books as Tolkien's *Lord of the Rings*. D & D succeeded beyond the developers' wildest expectations, with over a million sets of the rules—which gradually became more coherent and more complex as feedback from players was incorporated into new editions—sold in the next six years. But this was just the start.

It seemed inevitable that computers would get in on the act at some stage. Computer memory is the ideal tool for keeping track of the complicated rules, situations, and inventories that are part of fantasy games.

Back in the dim, dark days of the immediate past—before the era of microcomputers—access to computers was restricted and expensive. The only way you could use a computer was via a time-sharing system. You communicated with a vast, remote computer, via a noisy teletype keyboard. The computer was dealing—apparently simultaneously—with scores, perhaps hundreds, of other users. It talked back to you by printing on the teletype. It was slow, inconvenient, and unless you were lucky to be able to access such a computer from work or college, very expensive. Access charges around $80 to $100 an hour were not unusual. Pretty obviously, this meant that game-playing and game-writing on computers was a pastime very few had the opportunity to pursue.

Two programmers (Will Crowther and Don Woods) got around the expense problem simply by appropriating computer time—which should have been used for such mundane tasks as aiding with the statistical analysis of the results of physics experiments—and using it for their own entertainment.

Working in the language Fortran (a forerunner of the BASIC language on your microcomputer), Crowther and Woods entered into history by writing the program *Adventure.* It was a mammoth work, plunging the player into a vast underground labyrinth which could take months to solve. Hundreds of thousands of man-hours were lost across the country as computer personnel neglected their work in obsessive drives to work their way through the underground labyrinth.

The original *Adventure,* and similar programs which followed it, demanded big, big computer memories. Memory was expensive in those days, and the first microcomputers had amounts which seem niggardly to us now. Scott Adams, an *Adventure* admirer, decided he would make the program fit into a TRS-80. Predictably, scornful laughter greeted his announcement of this grandiose aim.

Fortunately, Scott succeeded, and on that base has built what is probably the world's leading computer adventure software company (Adventure International). The Adams material is available for most popular computers, and its usefulness is enhanced by a "difficulty rating" which is printed on each pack. *Pirate Adventure* is the easiest. The difficulty ratings go from beginner to medium difficulty and end up with the daunting "Advanced Adventurers Only Need Apply."

Once Adams had shown it was possible to squeeze an adventure into the mini-memory of a microcomputer, many others followed. Groups of users formed clubs to share ideas on solving problems.

Some of the most fanatical of these groups are those involved in the adventure program *Zork* (and, more recently, *Zork II* and *Zork III*), produced originally by a computer group at the Massachusetts Institute of Technology.

Most adventure games (including those in this book) invite the player to either enter a single letter (such as "N" meaning the player wishes to move north) or a two-word verb/noun phrase (such as SLAY DRAGON) to tell the computer what to do next. *Zork* and many other recent adventures accept multiple-statement inputs such as GET THE AXE AND DROP THE LAMP THEN GO NORTH. The *Zork* group publishes hint sheets and maps, and even bumper stickers (HONK IF YOU LOVE ZORK?).

There are several "classic" concepts which lie behind the development of adventure programs. I've tried to incorporate all of them into this book, so the ideas you pick up here can easily be applied to adventures from other sources.

First, a computer adventure is, in essence, a puzzle or series of puzzles. The puzzles are invented by the programmer, and must be solved by the player. The original *Adventure* and the Adams products are good examples of this.

When playing a computer adventure you must first discover the vocabulary the program will accept and understand, and then use this to explore your environment. Early adventures made much of battling monsters, gathering treasure and solving odd puzzles, such as trying to guess the code word which the "troll guarding the twisty bridge" would accept to let you pass.

The puzzles in my programs are far simpler than those you'll meet in commercial adventures, but serve as good training ground for your later explorations.

Computer adventurers soon learned that stable environments produced far more satisfactory adventures than did those in which the relationship between rooms, and the scenery, changed at the whim of the computer's random number generator. By stable, I mean an environment which has an inner consistency, and which—most importantly—can be mapped.

There is an immense amount of satisfaction to be gained from deducing the layout of the land in which you find yourself, and then in "wandering around it," checking out your map. All the environments in this book can be mapped.

The techniques discussed in this book for adventure development will not only help you create your own adventures, but should give you a number of ideas to help you solve adventures written by others.

Many educators bemoan the fact that little computer software of a truly educational nature has been developed. I believe that there is much educational value in the development and solving of adventure programs. Writing in the magazine *Popular Computing* (December 1983, pp. 147–150), Dr. Peter Owens, an English professor at Southeastern Massachusetts University, says that he has found that adventure games "satisfy a couple of requirements that give them validity as educational exercises." He then cites the engagement of thinking skills and the fact that the challenge of using imaginative approaches to problems can teach techniques which can be applied to real-life experiences.

So, there is an added bonus to adventure gaming. I think now it is time we buckled on our armor, conjured up a few soul-protection spells, and went down into the dungeons.

1

GIVE ME MY BOW

Let's face it. Life can be pretty tame, sometimes. There don't seem to be many dragons waiting to be slain in my city, and chests heaped high with abandoned gold are in scarce supply. I can't remember the last time I met an Evil Magician down at the local supermarket, and it's been ages since I discussed battle tactics with sentient androids at the local tavern.

The hunger for excitement lies in all of us. The desire to take on the personalities of other, more vibrant, people—even for just an hour or so—is a common one. Although you can't conjure up devils and werebears, envoke the power of a Shield of Protection, or employ trolls to carry sacks of emeralds from the ruins of an abandoned castle, role-playing games allow you to do just that.

Adventure gaming has hit the big time. You've probably seen the claims that it is the "fastest growing game in the world." Whether that's true or not, it indicates that Adventure gaming is a leisure pursuit which satisfies the inner needs of many people.

You may well have taken part in Adventure role-playing games yourself.

But these real-life campaigns have one enormous disadvantage. You need people to play with and against. You need a referee (often called the Game Master, or Dungeon Master) to control the world and its artifacts and encounters. It is not always particularly easy to get all these other human beings together just when you decide you'd like to indulge in a little bit of Adventuring.

That's where the computer comes into its own.

Although computer Adventure games lack a little of the spontaneity of games played with live company, they can be remarkably unpredictable and exciting to play. The fact that the Hydra of 10

Heads you've just slain exists only within your computer's RAM seems in no way to diminish the relief you feel when it dies. The gems you find lying all over the place are no less "real" than those discovered in live-action Adventures.

How to Read This Book

I've written this book to show you just how easy it is to create computer Adventure games of your own. However, there is one problem, and I hope you'll be willing to work with me to solve this problem. It is pretty difficult to know where to begin explaining how a computer Adventure is structured. Many times I've discovered that understanding one particular programming concept depends on your already understanding a second, separate concept. I've done all I can to make sure that the introduction of these concepts follows a more or less logical order and that all new concepts are carefully explained. Unfortunately, because of the complexity of most Adventure game programs, from time to time this has been impossible. All I can do is ask you to proceed on trust. Explanations which are not blindingly clear the first time you read them should swiftly fall into place as you continue working through the book.

I have written this work with the ancient Chinese maxim—A PROGRAM IS WORTH A THOUSAND WORDS—always in mind. You can learn far more by entering a program, or program fragment, and then running it, than you can from chapter after chapter of explanation. Therefore, this book is program-oriented. It contains four major programs (plus variations), and the instruction part of the book is based on these programs. In fact, if you just want some Adventure programs to run, you can just enter and run the programs as they are, ignoring the lucid explanations which surround them.

However, as is obvious, if you do this you'll miss the whole point of the book. Proceed slowly, have your computer running when you read, and enter each piece of code as you come to it, and you'll discover that in a very short while from now, you'll be creating Adventure programs of your own.

We'll begin with two quick looks at Adventure games in progress. Chapter 2 contains a version of the game WEREWOLVES AND WANDERER that you play by flipping two coins. If you haven't played an Adventure game before, this will give you a good idea of what to expect. Chapter 3 shows brief "snapshots" from the computerized version of WEREWOLVES AND WANDERER in action.

As I mentioned before, one of the most satisfying aspects of computer Adventuring, and therefore one of the most critical parts of Adventure programs, is the design or discovery of the computer-stored "map" of the environment that the Adventure takes place in. Chapter 4 shows how your computer can keep track of a floor plan for a deserted castle, or a dark dungeon, or whatever environment you choose.

In the next nine chapters (chapters 5 through 13) we begin our step-by-step construction of WEREWOLVES AND WANDERER. From this point on in the book you should enter the lines of the programs as they are given. This will teach you a great deal about how an Adventure program is written.

Chapters 14 and 15 show a more elaborate version of this program, creating a less predictable (and therefore more exciting) Adventure. You will discover a number of key ideas you can use to add interest to your own programs.

Next we will turn our original WEREWOLVES AND WANDERER program into a totally different Adventure, THE ASIMOVIAN DISASTER. Both versions of WEREWOLVES AND WANDERER take place within a deserted castle. THE ASIMOVIAN DISASTER takes place in outer space, where you (playing the part of an intrepid space explorer) have come upon the wreck of the giant space liner, *The Isaac Asimov*. You become trapped within the wreckage, and while avoiding crazed androids and unfriendly aliens, have to work your way to the Life Pod launching area, to get aboard the final Life Pod and blast your way to safety. This will serve as an excellent illustration of how a basic Adventure program can easily be adapted to simulate the environment and situation of *your* choice.

Finally, we'll present two completely different Adventure programs: THE CITADEL OF PERSHU and CHATEAU GAILLARD. These programs introduce more sophisticated Adventure programming techniques.

Adapting the Programs for Your Computer

I wrote the programs in this book on an IBM PC, but since many of you own or use different kinds of microcomputers, I've deliberately used only those parts of BASIC that will run on most microcomputers without changes. (The listings in this book are also fully compatible with Microsoft BASIC and MSX BASIC.)

You'll find no PEEKs and POKEs, no use of graphic character sets, and no use of such commands as SOUND or PLAY. I've assumed you have access to READ and DATA, and that your screen is around 40 characters wide (and you'll find, if you have a computer like the VIC-20 with a screen which is not that wide, it is fairly easy to adapt the program output to fit, as much of it consists of PRINT statements which can be abbreviated to comply with your computer's needs).

Of course, you'll probably have to play with the display a little, in order to make it as effective as possible. I expect, by the way, that you may well want to modify and adapt the programs to make the most of your system, adding sound and color, plus your own system's graphics, wherever you can.

Some of the BASIC statements used in the programs may have to be changed slightly to run on your system.

For example, if I want to generate random integers in the range, say, 1 to 10, I use a command of the type A = INT (RND(1)*10) + 1. When I want a number less than one, I've sometimes used just A = RND. If your system doesn't use this kind of random number statement you may have to substitute either A = RND(10) or A = INT (RND(0)*10) + 1 or A = INT (RND(1)*10) + 1 (you may well need to precede this with LET). You probably know exactly how to do it right now, but if you're not sure, look up RND or "random numbers" in your system's manual.

Although much of the output within quotation marks in PRINT statements is in lower-case, all programs accept input in upper-case letters. If your system does not have lower-case letters, simply put the material in PRINT statements in upper-case. It's been put in lower-case just because I think it looks better, but it has nothing to do with the actual running of the program.

Most computers allow line lengths of 255 characters or more. Others, such as the Commodore 64 and the VIC 20, have a limit (four lines for the 64, two lines for the 20). If your computer has a limit, and using abbreviations for keywords will not get the line in, you can usually split the line at any colon. If, however, the long lines test a number of conditions, you should use some of the IF/THEN tests in the first line to jump over the second set of IF/THENs (in an additional second line) with a GOTO if they are not met.

Note that some BASICs, such as Atari BASIC, do not support a string within an INPUT statement. Replace this with a PRINT "string" followed by a separate INPUT.

Some BASICs do not READ array values directly, as in READ A(7) or READ A$(7). Replace these with lines in which the data read is set equal to a variable, which is then made equal to the array element, as in READ X:A(7)=X or READ X$:A$(7)=X$.

If your computer does not support IF/THEN/ELSE, split it into two separate IF/THEN statements. For CLS (to clear the screen) use PRINT "CLR" on the Commodore machines and Atari computers, HOME on Apples, and CALL CLEAR when working with TI Extended BASIC. If you do not have INKEY$ on your computer, use either INPUT A$ or GET A$ (except in TI Extended BASIC, where you can use CALL KEY).

String-handling can cause a few problems, so I've deliberately kept it to a minimum in the programs in this book. If your computer does not support the standard string-handling commands of LEFT$, MID$ and RIGHT$, consult your manual. In TI Extended BASIC, SEG$(A$,2,3) replaces MID$(A$(2,3)), while A$(2 TO 5) should be used on Timex/Sinclair computers, and A$(2,5) when working in Atari BASIC.

Don't be intimidated by the length of this series of instructions. I've included these notes just to be sure that you can get the programs up and running as quickly as possible.

As you can see, certain microcomputers require special forms of the BASIC commands used in the programs in this book. The changes I've described above should cover most of the adaptations you'll have to make to get the programs running on your computer. You'll probably find, in fact, that when you get to entering the programs you'll automatically make the small changes needed to accommodate the special features of your system.

Please be sure to type the programs in carefully. Remember that the instructions you give to a computer must be exactly correct—or the machine won't be able to run your program. If you have trouble getting a program to run, first proofread your typed-in version against the listing given in this book.

Adapting or improving a program can be an excellent education in the mechanics of BASIC programming. The manual for the BASIC that comes with your computer is an indispensible tool. Check the manual to see what's wrong with any program lines that won't work—or that result in error messages. Make sure to use the exact form of the commands as given in the manual.

Talking to someone who has a lot of programming experience with the computer you use can be a tremendous help in solving any problems you might encounter. One of the wide range of books that explain introductory BASIC programming—including several devoted exclusively to the differences between the BASICs that work on different microcomputers—could also help.

It is impossible to predict exactly how much memory the programs will take on your system, because of the different ways memory is organized, and the working space the program requires differs from system to system.

The longer programs, especially THE CITADEL OF PERSHU and CHATEAU GAILLARD, take up a fair amount of memory: almost 20K for the first, and close to 25K for the second. If memory is in short supply on your system, see Chapter 19 for some hints on how to "compress" the amount of memory the programs require.

2

YOU ARE THE HERO

We'll start our investigation of Adventure gaming by allowing you to take part in an Adventure which does not need the computer.

The Adventure you will experience—WEREWOLVES AND WANDERER—is, in fact, based on the first program we will enter into the computer, and uses the same map, the same monsters, and much the same wording.

However, the computerless Adventure, in which you make decisions about what you want to do, where you want to go, and how you want to act, is not as satisfying as the computer version of the game we will develop. The main reason for presenting it in this book is to give you a feel for Adventure gaming, and especially for the program we are going to develop, without your first having to enter a very long program.

Many Adventure games make use of dice for determining the outcome of battles. As you may well not have dice lying conveniently around, our Adventure simply asks you to toss one or two coins, with the outcome of the toss deciding who has won a fight, and so on.

It is very simple to take part in this Adventure. You just follow the instructions, reading each section as you are directed to it, and then move to the new section indicated. For example, the text might read: "You come to a fork in the road. Turn to 84 if you want to turn right, to 12 if you want to turn left."

You turn to the indicated section, where new instructions (and choices) are waiting. In due course, you'll either complete the Adventure successfully, or you'll die in the attempt.

One of the real advantages of using a computer for Adventure gaming is that it can be used for all the "housekeeping" tasks. These include such things as rolling the dice and interpreting the outcome, keeping track of your score, of the number of monsters killed, the objects which are in the various locations you'll explore and in your backpack, and controlling the fights. This allows you to get on with the fun of actually enjoying the game, and allows you to let your imagination have full rein to fill in the background details and scenery for the Adventure.

Unfortunately, you'll have to do much of this housekeeping yourself in this first Adventure. The only equipment needed to take part is a pen and paper, this book, and two coins.

You start the game with $50 in gold, and a strength rating of 50. Your strength is diminished in certain battles, and the amount of gold and other treasure you have may change as you find gems lying around, you are robbed, or have to pay bribes. You die, and the game ends, if your strength falls below zero. From time to time you may well be told something like: "You lost that battle, your strength is halved." When you come across an instruction like that, divide your current strength rating by two, then round up to the nearest whole number. Don't worry about the fractions.

You'll have to keep a written tally of your strength and wealth, and the number of monsters you kill (this is called the "monster tally"). At the end of a game, you work out your score, which is based on the strength you have left, the money you have and the monsters you have killed.

IMPORTANT NOTE: Sometimes you'll be directed out of a room in the middle of a particular instruction. When you return to that room from that particular "subdirection," go to the part of the original description which is after the line which sent you to the subdirection. Otherwise, you'll be shuttling back and forth till the end of time.

The Scenario

This Adventure, WEREWOLVES AND WANDERER (where you are the wanderer, and the werewolves and other unsavory creatures inhabit the imaginary environment you are about to visit), takes place within an ancient, abandoned, stone castle.

You read about the castle in a faded letter you found in a trunk left to you by your grandfather. Unfortunately, you could only find the second page of the letter, so you are not sure of the full story. However, from the page remaining, you understand the castle was abandoned centuries ago after a curse was placed on the inhabitants by an old witch who had been evicted during a particularly harsh thunderstorm. The king's wife was ailing, and he (wrongly, as it turned out) blamed the witch for his wife's illness. He thought by throwing the witch out, her malignant influence on his wife would cease. This did not happen, and his wife became more and more ill, and finally died.

Her last days were not peaceful. The old woman's curse brought a reign of terror to the castle, as many odd creatures and ghosts took up residence within the castle. Finally, the king and his court could stand it no more, and they fled from their former home, never to be heard of again.

The creatures invoked by the witch stayed on, and are living there still. You are about to enter their realm.

The Choices

As I pointed out before, you start the game with $50 in gold, and a strength rating of 50. Take out your pen and paper, and head three columns as follows:

STRENGTH	WEALTH	MONSTER TALLY
50	50	0

All you have to do now, as you progress through the castle, aided only by your quick decisions and your two coins, is keep track of your progress. You'll find that you can take part in this adventure several times, as the outcome will be different each time. Keep a record of your final score, and see if you can better it each time you go exploring.

You start by proceeding straight to section 7:

1

You are in a dank, dark dungeon. The only light comes into the room from a small hole in the west wall. You must now flip a coin. If it lands heads, go to 11; tails, move to 5. To leave the dungeon, go to 25.

2

You are in the L-shaped upper hallway of the castle. A moth flutters across the room near the ceiling. To the north is a door and there is a stairwell in the hall as well. If you wish to peek through the door to the north, go to 33. If you wish to look down the stairwell, go to 39. You must flip a coin; if it lands tails, go to 13. To go through the door, go to 30. To go down the stairs, go to 21.

3

Looking down the stairwell, you can see a gloomy, unpleasant-looking room, the guardroom of the ancient dungeon. Go to 21.

4

Inside the sack you find jewels worth $500, so add them to your wealth and then go to 9.

5

The ghost of the guard has awoken! Your strength is halved due to the fright you suffered. Now go to 1.

6

You are in the Great Hall of the castle. There are two doors in the L-shaped room. You notice the wood panels around the room are warped and faded. As you look around, a mouse scampers across the floor. You whirl around at a sudden noise. Flip a coin. If it is heads, go to 43. If it is tails, you see to your relief there is nothing there. If you want to look out of the windows to get your bearings, go to 28. To exit by the north doors, go to 29. To move to the east, go to 21. Going to 29 will take you to the west.

7

You are at the entrance of a forbidding-looking stone castle. You are facing east. The huge wooden entrance door stands lightly open. To enter the castle, go to 40.

8

A werewolf awakes in this room. He attacks you. Flip a coin. If it is heads, the werewolf has beaten you, so go to 37. If it is tails, you have killed it. Add one to your monster tally, then go to 35.

9

You are in the storeroom, amidst spices, vegetables, and vast sacks of flour and other provisions. The air is thick with spice and curry fumes. If you want to look under some of the sacks, go to 31. If you want to look inside the top sack, go to 4. To leave by the south door, go to 42. Go to 35 if you wish to leave by the north door.

10

Looking up the stairwell you can just make out an elaborately decorated hallway. Go to 21.

11

There are rats in this dungeon. They steal gold pieces worth $10 from you. Go to 1.

12

You are descending very, very slowly. Your strength is sapped by a magic spell left in the elevator. Divide your strength by two, then proceed straight to 42.

13

A malevolent Maldemer attacks you. You can smell the sulfur on his breath. Your strength diminishes by 10. Flip two coins. If they both come up heads, you have killed the Maldemer, so add one to your monster tally. After the battle, go to 42.

14

You've done it! That was the exit from the castle. Double your strength, then go to 27.

15

You are in the castle's ancient, hydraulic elevator. If you wish to descend slowly, go to 12. To get down as quickly as possible, go to 24.

16

Horrors. There is a devastating Ice-Dragon here. It leaps toward you. Blood drips from his claws. Flip a coin. Heads you win, adding one to your monster tally. Your strength drops by 10 if you win; by 20 if you lose. After the fight, go to 30.

17

This is the monarch's private meeting room. The echo of ancient plotting and wrangling hangs heavy in the musty air. Flip a coin. If it lands up heads, you find an emerald worth $100, then go to 21, the exit through the south door. If it is tails, you are attacked by a ghastly Gruesomeness which was hiding behind the drapes. Flip the coin again. If it lands tails again, you win, adding one to your monster tally. If it lands heads, the Gruesomeness wins. While you are lying exhausted on the floor, he steals $100 from your wealth. Now go to 21.

18

This tiny room on the upper level is the dressing chamber. There is a window to the north. If you wish to see out the window, go to 22. There is a door which leaves the room to the south. To use this door, go to 32.

19

The noise is frightening. What on earth (or beyond it) is inside that room? Go to 23.

20

Aha . . . wealth! You find great treasure here worth $900 in gems and gold. Add it to your wealth, then go to 30.

21

You are in the inner hallway, which contains a door to the north, one to the west, and a circular stairwell. The room is small and unfriendly. To look down the stairwell, go to 3. To look up the stairs, go to 10. To leave by the north door, go to 17. Go to 6 if you wish to leave by the west door. Go to 2 to go up the stairs, or to 25 to go down them.

22

Looking out the window you see, below you, the secret herb garden. Looking hard to the left, you recognize the land you crossed to get to the castle entrance. Now go to 18.

23

You are in the room which was used as the castle treasury years ago. A spider scampers down the wall. There are no windows, just exits to the north and to the east. If you wish to listen at the north door, go to 19. If you want to leave by the north door, go to 32. Go to 36 to leave by the east door.

24

You feel exhilarated, as a positive spell is triggered by your swift downward flight. Your strength is doubled. Now go to 42.

25

You are in the prison guardroom, in the basement of the castle. The stairwell ends in this room. There is one other exit, a small hole in the east wall. The air is damp and unpleasant . . . a chill wind rushes into the room from gaps in the stone at the top of the walls. To go east, go to 1. To go up the stairs, go to 21.

26

Looking out the south window you see the ornamental lake. There is a view across open fields through the east window. You look longingly at the outdoors, then go to 42.

27

Your score is five times your strength, plus two times your wealth, plus thirty times your monster tally. You have come to the end of the adventure. Now proceed with the rest of this book.

28

By straining your eyes through the mist which has swirled up while you've been exploring, you can see below you, looking southwards, an ornamental lake. By craning your neck round to the right through the west window you can just see the entrance door to the castle. When you've finished looking, go to 6.

29

You are in the castle's Audience Chamber. The faded tapestries on the wall only hint at the splendor which this room once had. There is a window to the west. By craning your neck through it to the right you can see the castle entrance. Flip two coins. If they both land heads, you find diamonds worth $169. If they are both tails, you must fight the fanatical Fleshgorger which suddenly stumbles into the room. To fight the Fleshgorger, flip both coins again. One head and one tail, you defeat it, adding one to your monster tally and doubling your strength. If the two coins are heads or tails, you lose, and your strength is halved. To leave by the north, go to 40. To leave by the south or the east doors, go to 6.

30

You find yourself in the master bedroom on the upper level of the castle. Looking down from the window to the west you can see the entrance to the castle, while the secret herb garden is visible below the north window. There are doors to the east and to the south. You must flip a coin. If it lands heads, go to 20. Go to 16 if it comes up tails. To leave by the south door, go to 2. Go to 32 if you wish to leave by the east door.

31

A ferocious werewolf leaps at you, his eyes glinting violently. Flip two coins, quickly. If they are the same, you defeat the werewolf. Although your strength is diminished by ten, you manage to escape, and go to 9. If the coins are different, the werewolf starts tearing you apart, cutting your strength to half of what it was before. You drag yourself away, and go to 9.

32

Oooh . . . you are in the chambermaid's bedroom. Faint perfume hangs in the air. There is an exit to the west and a door to the south. However, your attention is caught by the steady thumping coming from behind the bed. Fearfully, you look behind it, and a devastating Ice-dragon leaps at you! You smell the sulfur on his breath. Flip two coins. Unless they are two heads, you lose, and 15 is struck from your strength tally. If you win, add 100 to your strength. To leave by the north, go to 18. Go to 30 if you wish to leave by the west door. The south door leads to 23.

33

Peering into the room you see it was once the master bedroom. It appears quiet. As you turn back you notice a small bottle on the ground. Quickly, you uncork it and swallow the contents. Flip two coins. Unless they are both tails, the bottle contained a wonderful elixir which has tripled your strength. If the coins were both tails, the bottle contained only water. Now go to 2.

34

Now you're under attack from a nasty, ghastly Gruesomeness. Flip two coins. Two tails, you win, and add 50 to your strength. Two heads, your strength is halved as the G.G. defeats you. Now go to 2.

35

This is the castle's kitchen. Through windows in the north wall you can see the secret herb garden. It has been many years since meals were prepared here for the monarch and the court. A rat scurries across the floor. Flip a coin. If it lands heads, you stumble, making a noise, and must go to 8 to see the effect that noise has had. To leave by the south door, go to 9.

36

You are in a small room which is outside the castle itself. You can see the lake through the southern windows. Flip a coin. If it is heads, go to 41. To leave by the north door, go to 15. Go to 23 if you wish to leave by the west door.

37

You are dead!!! Go to 27.

38

Go to 14

39

Looking down the stairwell you can see a small room below, and on the floor below that, you can just make out the gloomy guardroom. A ghost of a former guardsman suddenly appears on the stairwell. He demands $100. If you have it, pay him, then go to 2. If you do not have enough, the guard attacks you in anger. Flip a coin. Heads, go to 37. Tails, halve your strength, then go to 2.

40

You are in the hallway entrance to the castle. It is dark and gloomy, and the air of decay and desolation is very depressing. You suddenly feel very frightened. To run away from the castle, go to 7. To proceed through the south door, go to 29.

41

A spider bites you on the leg. Your strength is diminished by 20. Now go to 36.

42

You are in the rear vestibule. There are windows to the south. To look out them, go to 26. Flip a coin. If it lands heads, go to 13. To leave by the north door, go to 9. Go to 38 to leave by the east door.

43

The horrendous Hodgepodge attacks you!!! He fights wildly, madly. Flip two coins. Unless they are both tails, you have beaten it, and double your strength. If they are both tails, the H.H. beats you, and your strength is halved. Now go to 6.

Once you've played this game a few times, you're certain to have a much better idea of how Adventures "feel," even though this coin-operated Adventure is a very pale shadow of the interactive enjoyment you'll experience when you get the programs up and running on your computer.

3

THE ADVENTURE IN ACTION

Before we look at our first Adventure listing in detail, spelling out each element of its development, I'll show you some "snapshots" of it in action. This should help you make sense of the various elements of the program as they are presented.

First the program asks your name, which it will use from time to time throughout the game:

```
WHAT IS YOUR NAME, EXPLORER? ANDREW
```

The computer then proceeds to tell you—as it will after each action you initiate—your current status:

```
ANDREW, YOUR STRENGTH IS 95
YOU HAVE $ 75
IT IS TOO DARK TO SEE ANYTHING

WHAT DO YOU WANT TO DO? I
```

The question "WHAT DO YOU WANT TO DO" is asked after every move. The answers the computer understands will be explained a little later under the heading "Vocabulary." Note here that our hero, Andrew, has entered "I," which stands for "inventory." This means he wants to add to his supplies of provisions.

The computer goes to the relevant subroutine where Andrew's money is shown ("YOU HAVE $75") and then the list of available products and their prices is shown:

```
PROVISIONS & INVENTORY

YOU HAVE $ 75

YOU CAN BUY 1 - FLAMING TORCH ($15)
            2 - AXE ($10)
            3 - SWORD ($20)
            4 - FOOD ($2 PER UNIT)
            5 - MAGIC AMULET ($30)
            6 - SUIT OF ARMOR ($50)
            0 - TO CONTINUE ADVENTURE
ENTER NO. OF ITEM REQUIRED? 1
```

Andrew enters a "1," telling the computer he wants to buy a "flaming torch" (item 1 on the inventory menu). The torch is added to his possessions, his wealth is decreased by $15, the cost of the torch, and the menu option is shown again:

```
YOU CAN BUY 1 - FLAMING TORCH ($15)
            2 - AXE ($10)
            3 - SWORD ($20)
            4 - FOOD ($2 PER UNIT)
            5 - MAGIC AMULET ($30)
            6 - SUIT OF ARMOR ($50)
            0 - TO CONTINUE ADVENTURE
ENTER NO. OF ITEM REQUIRED? 4
HOW MANY UNITS OF FOOD? 20
```

This time, Andrew has chosen item 4 on the menu, signifying that he wants to buy food. Food is a very valuable possession. You start the game with a limited amount of strength, which is gradually consumed as the game goes on. If it drops to zero, you die, and the game ends. Fights against wild monsters also diminish your strength. Eating food replenishes it. You have to keep an eye on your current "strength rating" throughout the game, and always make sure you have food on hand to replenish your rating when needed.

After entering item 4 on the menu, Andrew is asked how much food he wants to buy, with each unit of food costing $2. After this purchase has been made (Andrew buys 20 units), he enters a 0 next time the menu is presented, indicating that he wishes to continue with the Adventure:

```
YOU HAVE $ 20

YOU CAN BUY 1 - FLAMING TORCH ($15)
            2 - AXE ($10)
            3 - SWORD ($20)
            4 - FOOD ($2 PER UNIT)
            5 - MAGIC AMULET ($30)
            6 - SUIT OF ARMOR ($50)
            0 - TO CONTINUE ADVENTURE
ENTER NO. OF ITEM REQUIRED? 0
```

Another status report is given, showing Andrew's strength and wealth, and the fact that his provisions sack holds 20 units of food. The location is described, and Andrew enters "E" (meaning he wants to move east) when asked what he wants to do next:

```
ANDREW, YOUR STRENGTH IS 90
YOU HAVE $ 20
YOUR PROVISIONS SACK HOLDS 20 UNITS OF FOOD

********************************

YOU ARE AT THE ENTRANCE TO A FORBIDDING-LOOKING
STONE CASTLE. YOU ARE FACING EAST

WHAT DO YOU WANT TO DO? E
```

He is moved eastwards, and another status report is given. Notice that his strength rating has been reduced slightly:

```
ANDREW, YOUR STRENGTH IS 85
YOU HAVE $ 20
YOUR PROVISIONS SACK HOLDS 20 UNITS OF FOOD

*********************************


YOU ARE IN THE HALLWAY
THERE IS A DOOR TO THE SOUTH
THROUGH WINDOWS TO THE NORTH YOU CAN SEE A SECRET
HERB GARDEN
THERE IS TREASURE HERE WORTH $ 100


WHAT DO YOU WANT TO DO? P
```

He sees that there is $100 worth of treasure here, so enters "P" (for "pick up the treasure") and when the status report comes back, the extra wealth has been added:

```
ANDREW, YOUR STRENGTH IS 80
YOU HAVE $ 120
YOUR PROVISIONS SACK HOLDS 20 UNITS OF FOOD

*********************************


YOU ARE IN THE HALLWAY
THERE IS A DOOR TO THE SOUTH
THROUGH WINDOWS TO THE NORTH YOU CAN SEE A SECRET
HERB GARDEN

WHAT DO YOU WANT TO DO? S
```

Moving south (he entered "S"), Andrew finds himself in the Audience Chamber. But he is not alone! His first battle is only moments away:

```
THIS IS THE AUDIENCE CHAMBER
THERE IS A WINDOW TO THE WEST. BY LOOKING TO THE
RIGHT
THROUGH IT YOU CAN SEE THE ENTRANCE TO THE CASTLE.
DOORS LEAVE THIS ROOM TO THE NORTH, EAST AND SOUTH

      DANGER...THERE IS A MONSTER HERE....

      IT IS A DEVASTATING ICE-DRAGON

      THE DANGER LEVEL IS 20 !!

      WHAT DO YOU WANT TO DO? F
```

Andrew has entered "F" (for "fight") when asked what he wants to do. He could have entered "R" (for "run") if he felt cowardly. However, the computer would not necessarily have accepted this, and may have told him "NO, YOU MUST STAND AND FIGHT". However, Andrew has decided not to try and run, but instead to battle the Ice-Dragon:

```
YOU HAVE NO WEAPONS
YOU MUST FIGHT WITH BARE HANDS


YOU ATTACK
```

```
YOU MANAGE TO WOUND IT

THE MONSTER WOUNDS YOU!

YOU ATTACK

YOU MANAGE TO WOUND IT

THE MONSTER WOUNDS YOU!
YOU ATTACK

AND YOU MANAGED TO KILL THE DEVASTATING ICE-DRAGON
```

His strength is failing, so he decides he must eat, so enters a "C" (for "consume"):

```
ANDREW, YOUR STRENGTH IS 65
YOU HAVE $ 120
YOUR PROVISIONS SACK HOLDS 20 UNITS OF FOOD

WHAT DO YOU WANT TO DO? C

YOU HAVE 20 UNITS OF FOOD
HOW MANY DO YOU WANT TO EAT? 15

ANDREW, YOUR STRENGTH IS 125
YOU HAVE $ 120
YOUR PROVISIONS SACK HOLDS 5 UNITS OF FOOD
```

And so the Adventure unfolds:

```
THIS ROOM WAS USED AS THE CASTLE TREASURY IN
BY-GONE YEARS....
```

```
THERE ARE NO WINDOWS, JUST EXITS TO THE
NORTH AND TO THE EAST
THERE IS TREASURE HERE WORTH $ 159


WHAT DO YOU WANT TO DO? P


ANDREW, YOUR STRENGTH IS 120
YOU HAVE $ 279
YOUR PROVISIONS SACK HOLDS 5 UNITS OF FOOD

********************************


THERE ARE NO WINDOWS, JUST EXITS TO THE
NORTH AND TO THE EAST


WHAT DO YOU WANT TO DO? E


_______________________________________


ANDREW, YOUR STRENGTH IS 115
YOU HAVE $ 279
YOUR PROVISIONS SACK HOLDS 5 UNITS OF FOOD

********************************


THIS IS THE SMALL ROOM OUTSIDE THE CASTLE
LIFT WHICH CAN BE ENTERED BY A DOOR TO THE NORTH
ANOTHER DOOR LEADS TO THE WEST. YOU CAN SEE
THE LAKE THROUGH THE SOUTHERN WINDOWS


WHAT DO YOU WANT TO DO? N
```

```
YOU HAVE ENTERED THE LIFT...
IT SLOWLY DESCENDS...
```

These "snapshots" from the game indicate clearly how the game behaves when the program is up and running. I hope you are now straining at the bit to get your first Adventure up and running.

4

CREATING THE FLOOR PLAN

In this chapter we will examine the critical problem of how to get your computer to keep track of the complicated "floor plan" or "map" used in an Adventure game. We'll take a careful look at how to write a program that keeps track of a simple five-room environment. Note that the program sections in this chapter refer only to this simplified environment, and are *not* part of WEREWOLVES AND WANDERER. Follow through the explanations and examples carefully. The concepts outlined here will later be expanded for use in our first full-scale Adventure program, WEREWOLVES AND WANDERER.

Mapping the Environment

As was pointed out earlier, an Adventure environment must be coherent. That is, the explorer making his way through the environment must be able to draw up a complete map as he works his way through it. If he draws a door connecting the study with the library on an environment floor plan, because he has discovered that going through the study door leads into the library, he is entitled to expect that turning around and going back will bring him back into the study. The game-player should be able to build up an entire plan in this way, checking his plan from time to time by "walking around" the house, castle, forest, underground labyrinth, or whatever where the Adventure is taking place.

The first step, then, in building an Adventure program is to construct an environment which can be both mapped, and represented in some way which the computer can store.

You'll be pleased to know it is relatively easy to satisfy both these conditions.

Look at the following five-room environment, a very simple one, which we shall treat as though it was a computer Adventure environment.

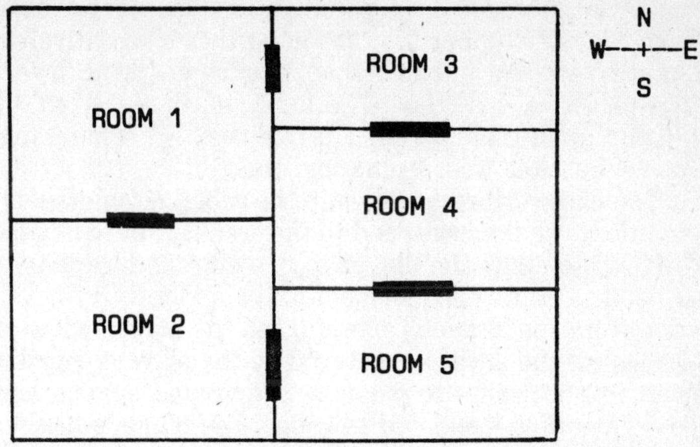

The key to holding an environment like this in a way the computer can understand and manipulate is to set up an array, each element of which represents a room. The solid markers between rooms are doors.

If you were in room one, you could move east into room three, or south into room two. In room four you can move north into room three and south into room five, and so on. Imagine we have set up an array, which we have dimensioned as DIM A(5,4). The first dimension is the room, and the second one is the four possible directions from that room (that is, north, south, east, and west).

Building a Travel Table

Armed with the map of the five-room environment, we can now build up a Travel Table, which can then be fed into the array, to allow us to move from point to point within the environment.

Here's the Travel Table for the simple, five-room environment:

ROOM	N	S	E	W
1	0	2	3	0
2	1	0	5	0
3	0	4	0	1
4	3	5	0	0
5	4	0	0	2

Take some time to study this table, and the way it relates to the map, because it is the single most important key to building Adventure programs you will learn from this book.

Look at the table for room one. Under the "N" (for north) column we see a zero, meaning you cannot move north from room one (a fact which is easily verified by looking at our map). However, under the "S" we see the number two, meaning that if we traveled south from room one we would end up in room two (again, you can verify this from the map). Move east (the "E" column, of course) from room one, and you'll end up in room three. The 0 in the "W" column means there is no travel possible west from room one.

You can work right through the table, if you like, checking that the numbers on it correspond to the "reality" of the map.

Now, to allow the player to move around the environment, we only need to (a) fill each element of the array with the relevant information from the Travel Table; (b) tell the player where he or she is; and (c) allow the decisions entered by the player regarding the direction he or she wants to move to be checked against the array, and then—if possible—updated to reflect the player's new location. It is easier to do this than you might think.

Moving About

Firstly, we need to write a small program to feed the relevant information into the array. Two simple READ/DATA loops like the following will do it:

```
10  DIM A(5,4)
20  FOR B = 1 TO 5
30  FOR C = 1 TO 4
40  READ A(B,C)
50  NEXT C
60  NEXT B
70  DATA 0,2,3,0
80  DATA 1,0,5,0
90  DATA 0,4,0,1
100 DATA 3,5,0,0
110 DATA 4,0,0,2
```

As you can see, the DATA statements correspond exactly with the items in our Travel Table.

This will fill the A array as follows:

```
A(1,1) = 0
A(1,2) = 2
A(1,3) = 3
A(1,4) = 4

A(2,1) = 1
A(2,2) = 0
A(2,3) = 5
A(2,4) = 0

A(3,1) = 0
A(3,2) = 4
A(3,3) = 0
A(3,4) = 1

A(4,1) = 3
A(4,2) = 5
A(4,3) = 0
A(4,4) = 0

A(5,1) = 4
A(5,2) = 0
A(5,3) = 0
A(5,4) = 2
```

Looking at these, we can see that the first number which comes after the A is the room number, and the second is the room the player ends up in if he or she moves in a direction where the first direction is north, the second is south, the third of course is east, and the final direction is west. This is all suggested by our Travel Table. I hope by now you are beginning to appreciate just how central the Travel Table is to constructing and manipulating an artificial environment.

The Player's Location

If we decided that the room the player is currently occupying could be designated by the variable RO (as we do, in fact, use in both WEREWOLVES AND WANDERER and THE ASIMOVIAN DISASTER), we could tell the player where he or she was as follows, as well as indicating which exits existed:

```
100  PRINT "YOU ARE IN ROOM NUMBER ";RO
110  IF A(RO,1) <> 0 THEN PRINT "A DOOR LEADS
     NORTH"
```

```
120  IF A(RO,2) <> 0 THEN PRINT "THERE IS AN
     EXIT TO THE SOUTH"
130  IF A(RO,3) <> 0 THEN PRINT "YOU CAN LEAVE
     VIA THE EAST EXIT"
140  IF A(RO,4) <> 0 THEN PRINT "A DOORWAY OPENS
     TO THE WEST"
```

The player's input could be a single letter ("N" for north, and so on) and the program could look at the input, and check to see if an exit to that direction existed:

```
150  INPUT "WHICH DIRECTION";D$
160  IF D$ = "N" AND A(RO,1) = 0 THEN PRINT
     "YOU CANNOT MOVE THAT WAY"
170  IF D$ = "S" AND A(RO,2) = 0 THEN PRINT
     "YOU CAN'T WALK THROUGH WALLS"
180  IF D$ = "E" AND A(RO,3) = 0 THEN PRINT
     "TRY ANOTHER DIRECTION"
190  IF D$ = "W" AND A(RO,4) = 0 THEN PRINT
     "THERE IS NO DOOR TO THE WEST"
```

As you'll see shortly, exactly this system is used in our Adventure programs.

So you can see how the array, constructed using the Travel Table, can indicate where the player may or may not move. What about the movement itself?

Moving Around the Map

The "you can't move that way" tests, of lines 160 to 190, could trigger a repeat of the input question, "WHICH DIRECTION?," over and over again until a valid direction was entered. Then the movement itself could take place. (Note, by the way, that the room numbers are never referred to explicitly, as they are for the computer's internal use only; all the player hears about are names of rooms—YOU ARE IN THE COUNTING HOUSE—and, in many cases, the contents of the room, and possible exits from it.)

If the player entered "N" (for north), as he or she was in room four (look to the map, to see what this would mean) the computer could proceed as follows. Firstly, the variable RO would equal 4. A short routine could convert the "N" into a 1 (for the first element of the array), so the computer would know the player was about to go into the room number A(RO,1). As RO equals 4, A(4,1) gives 3. This means the player would be moving into room number 3 (which, as a quick check of the map will reveal, is north of room 4). The variable RO would be set equal to three, so the player could be told "YOU ARE IN ROOM 3." The next choice of direction could then be entered, and so the player would continue happily tripping through the environment.

Consistency and Reality

Although the rooms only exist on paper and in elements in an array, the fact that they behave like "real rooms" soon allows them to be perceived as though they were solid and real in a way which is uncanny. Add descriptions of each room—YOU ARE IN A SMALL WORKMAN'S HUT ATTACHED TO THE BACK OF THE MANOR HOUSE, WITH A PILE OF STRAW OVER IN THE FAR CORNER, AND A SHOVEL AND AN AXE LYING UNDERNEATH THE WINDOW. A LARGE LOAF OF BREAD IS ON THE TABLE, AND BESIDE IT IS A NOTE. DOORS LEAVE TO THE NORTH AND TO THE WEST—and you'll find the environment takes on quite solid dimensions in your mind.

Once the map becomes more complex, as in WEREWOLVES AND WANDERER (and to a much greater extent in THE ASIMOVIAN DISASTER), and the descriptions help clarify the mental images of the rooms, you'll find you have a counterfeit reality with immense power in your hands.

You might like to try and write a simple program, before proceeding further, which allows you to move around the five-room environment we've been looking at.

5

CREATING THE STRUCTURE

We'll move now from considering the simple, five-room environment, to the much more complex (19 rooms in all) castle environment you will inhabit when taking the part of the Wanderer in WEREWOLVES AND WANDERER. Let's begin with an explanation of how such a complicated program is designed.

The Master Loop

This Adventure program is structured according to a well-defined outline, which was drawn up long before the castle floor plan was created, or any of the incidents which would occur during the playing of the game were considered. Working to an outline like this, in which the actions the program must take are determined before any attention is given to the actual form or coding of the program, is often called "structured programming." This is discussed in some detail in Chapter 23, but it is appropriate to introduce it briefly at this point. The original WEREWOLVES AND WANDERER outline looked like this, before any program was actually written:

```
MAIN HANDLING ROUTINE
    INFORM PLAYER OF ROOM CONTENTS AND OWN
      STATUS
    PICK UP TREASURE
    FIGHT MONSTER
    EAT FOOD
    BUY PROVISIONS

IF PLAYER STILL ALIVE AND NOT EXIT, GO TO MAIN
HANDLING ROUTINE AGAIN
```

CONGRATULATE OR OTHERWISE

END

The program consisted only of this bare outline at the beginning. Finally, the program ended up as follows. You can see that the bare outline has strongly controlled the final structure of the program:

IDENTIFY (line 10)

GOTO INITIALIZATION ROUTINE (20)

GOSUB MAJOR HANDLING ROUTINE (30)

IF PLAYER HAS NOT BEEN KILLED, OR REACHED THE EXIT, GO BACK TO THE LINE ABOVE WHICH SENDS ACTION TO THE MAJOR HANDLING ROUTINE (40)

CONGRATULATIONS MESSAGE (70–140)

MAJOR HANDLING ROUTINE (160–320)

IF PLAYER HAS LIGHT, DESCRIBE ROOM (330)

CHECK FOR MONSTERS/TREASURE, DESCRIBE (360–440)

ASK FOR PLAYER'S MOVE (450–710)

FIGHT SUBROUTINE (720–970)

ROOM DESCRIPTION SUBROUTINES (990–2280)

DEATH MESSAGE (2300–2330)

PICK UP TREASURE ROUTINE (2350–2400) TELL COWARD PLAYER HE OR SHE MUST FIGHT (2420–2460)

EAT FOOD, INCREASE STRENGTH (2480–2580)

INITIALIZE (2600–2990)
- ASSIGN VARIABLES
- FILL FLOOR PLAN ARRAY
- GET PLAYER'S NAME
- ALLOT TREASURE TO ROOMS

ALLOT MONSTERS TO ROOMS

INVENTORY/PROVISIONS SUBROUTINE (3010–3290)

DATA STATEMENTS FOR FLOOR PLAN (3310–3490)

DELAY LOOP (3520–3530)

Now that you've seen the overall structure, you should be able to appreciate that writing at least an initial outline helps give form to a program which could otherwise easily get out of control.

The program sits within a "master loop" which calls all the needed subroutines, then checks to see if the game is over (because the player has reached the exit, or is dead). If this check is negative (that is, the player is not dead, and the final exit has not been found), the program loops back to go through it all again. This cycle continues until one of the "end condition" tests proves positive.

Modular Construction

The program was written in a series of discrete modules, a process I strongly suggest you follow. It will help you keep a long and complex program under control, when a less disciplined approach would make the task almost impossible. A program which is constructed in modules is also much easier to modify (as you'll see when we look at the more elaborate form of WEREWOLVES AND WANDERER) and debug. To make it easier to keep track of the separate modules, they are divided by a REM statement full of asterisks, so the separate modules are immediately visible when you look at the listing as a whole.

The program begins, then, with these four lines:

```
10 REM WEREWOLVES AND WANDERER
20 GOSUB 2600:REM INITIALISE
30 GOSUB 160
40 IF RO <> 11 THEN 30
```

If RO equals 11, the game is over, as room eleven is the final exit from the castle. As you can see, line 20 calls the subroutine which starts at line 2600, the initialization subroutine. Line 30 calls the Major Handling Routine, and if the check in line 40 proves negative, goes back to 30 to call this routine again.

6

THE ENVIRONMENT UNFOLDS

The Initializing Subroutine

As you saw at the end of the last chapter, line 20 sends action to the initializing subroutine which begins at line 2600. Here it is:

```
2590 REM ***********
2600 REM INITIALISE
2670 REM **************
2680 REM SET UP CASTLE
2690 DIM A(19,7)
2700 FOR B=1 TO 19
2710 FOR C=1 TO 7
2720 READ A(B,C)
2730 NEXT C
2740 NEXT B
```

These are the lines which fill the array with the numbers which represent the directions the player can move from various rooms.

The seventh element for each room is used to hold either treasure or terror, as will be explained in the next chapter.

In this game, there are six possible directions, the four compass points as well as up and down. The castle has three levels, and you are able to move from one to the next via a circular stairwell, and "an ancient hydraulic lift." The numbers which follow the DATA statements (lines 3310 to 3490) represent, for each room: north, south, east, west, up and down. Here they are:

```
3300 REM ******************
3310 DATA 0,2,0,0,0,0,0:REM ROOM 1
3320 DATA 1,3,3,0,0,0,0:REM ROOM 2
3330 DATA 2,0,5,2,0,0,0:REM ROOM 3
3340 DATA 0,5,0,0,0,0,0:REM ROOM 4
3350 DATA 4,0,0,3,15,13,0:REM ROOM 5
3360 DATA 0,0,1,0,0,0,0: REM ROOM 6
3370 DATA 0,8,0,0,0,0,0: REM ROOM 7
3380 DATA 7,10,0,0,0,0,0: REM ROOM 8
3390 DATA 0,19,0,8,0,8,0:REM ROOM 9
3400 DATA 8,0,11,0,0,0,0:REM ROOM 10
3410 DATA 0,0,10,0,0,0,0:REM ROOM 11
3420 DATA 0,0,0,13,0,0,0:REM ROOM 12
3430 DATA 0,0,12,0,5,0,0:REM ROOM 13
3440 DATA 0,15,17,0,0,0,0:REM ROOM 14
3450 DATA 14,0,0,0,0,5,0:REM ROOM 15
3460 DATA 17,0,19,0,0,0,0:REM ROOM 16
3470 DATA 18,16,0,14,0,0,0:REM ROOM 17
3480 DATA 0,17,0,0,0,0,0:REM ROOM 18
3490 DATA 9,0,16,0,0,0,0:REM ROOM 19
```

The Maps

We must see now how they relate to the floor plan of the castle. Of course, when you give this game to somebody to play you do not provide them with a map. Part of the pleasure of playing Adventure is constructing a map of the environment which will give you control of it. "Walking through" an environment when you have mapped it, to check your cartographic work, is also part of the fun. The map is only given here so you can see how the program relates to it.

There are, as I said, three levels. The basement is made up of a guard room, and a dungeon, like this:

The ground floor, where you begin your quest, looks like this:

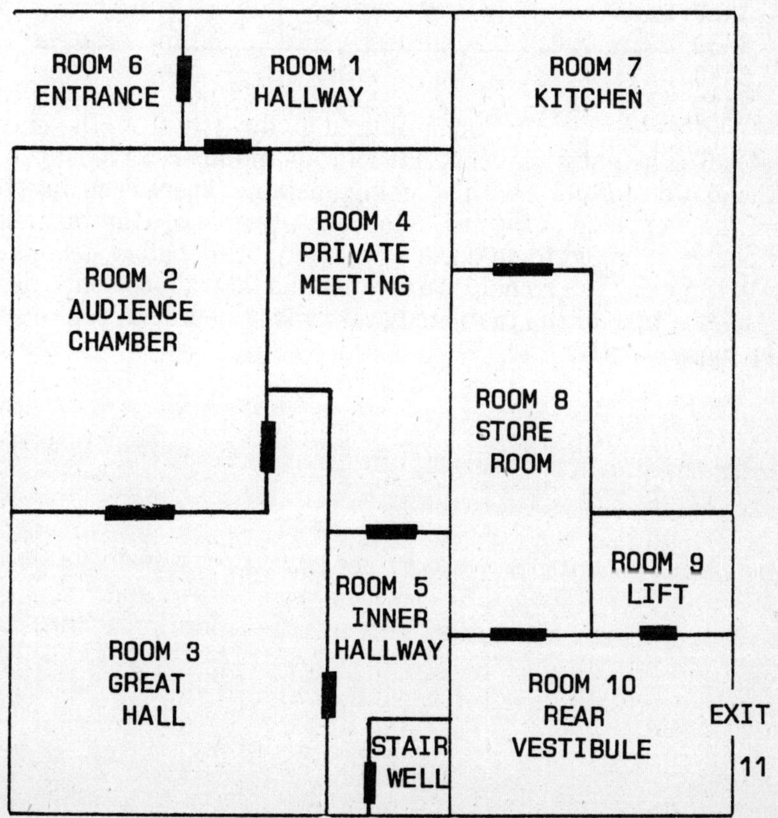

And the upper floor is built as follows:

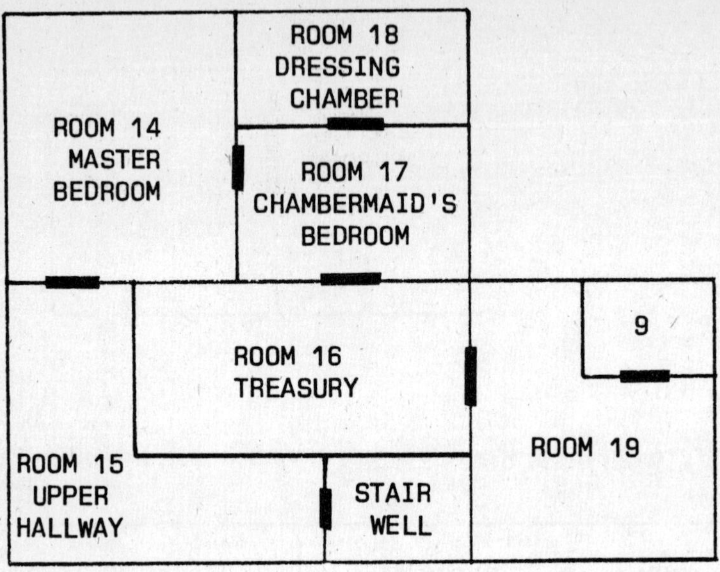

You'll see that it is impossible to go directly from the entrance ("room 6": the entrance must have a room number, as must the exit) to the exit ("room 11") without going upstairs. There is no direct path from the west side of the castle to the eastern one. This ensures that the player is forced to do quite a bit of exploring before being able to locate the exit. It also helps to confuse the map a bit. Constructing a three-level map of the castle may take many hours, as you're sure to appreciate shortly.

7

TREASURE AND TERROR

Now that we have created a section of program to handle the physical environment of the castle in a form which we can manipulate, we need to fill some of the rooms, so the player will have treasure to find and monsters to battle.

Distributing the Treasure

This is easy to do. Let's look at adding treasure for a start. Here is the section of code required:

```
2830 REM **************
2840 REM ALLOT TREASURE
2850 FOR J = 1 TO 4
2860 M=INT(RND(1)*19)+1
2870 IF M=6 OR M=11 OR A(M,7)<>0 THEN 28
60
2880 A(M,7)=INT(RND(1)*100)+10
2890 NEXT J
```

Lines 2860 and 2870 choose a room number between 1 and 19, check that it is not 6 (the entrance, outside the castle) or 11 (the exit, outside), and then check that this room is empty. You will recall we mentioned in the last chapter that the seventh element for each room was left blank to allow for contents. Now we are filling it. If this element is zero, the room is currently empty.

Once a room has been chosen with line 2860, line 2880 puts an amount of money in it between $10 and $109.

Distributing the Monsters

With the treasure in place, it is time to allot our terrors. The next routine does this, choosing a room in the same way as our money routine did, then setting that element equal to a negative number (−1 to −4):

```
2900 REM ***************
2910 REM ALLOT MONSTERS
2920 FOR J = 1 TO 4
2930 M=INT(RND(1)*18)+1
2940 IF M=6 OR M=11 OR A(M,7)<>0 THEN 29
30
2950 A(M,7)= -J
2960 NEXT J
```

You can see now that if the computer looks at the seventh element of a room, it can tell if it is empty (equals 0), contains treasure (greater than 9) or a monster (less than 1) and can give the player a message to this effect. Extending the use of the room array in this way points up again how vital the array is to the construction and control of an Adventure environment.

Finally, we put treasure in two rooms (the Private Meeting Room and the Treasury) regardless of whether the above routines have already put anything there. These lines wipe over anything else which has been placed there:

```
2970 A(4,7)=100+INT(RND(1)*100)
2980 A(16,7)=100+INT(RND(1)*100)
2990 RETURN
```

The RETURN line, of course, is simply used to terminate the initialization subroutine.

Adding Variables

A number of variables are needed to add to the creation of a realistic Adventure environment. I make it a practice to use explicit variable names which will remind me (or tell me straight out) what the variable stands for. Many computer systems only recognize the first two letters of a variable name, so I have made sure in this program (and the others in the book) that the same first two letters are not used for different variables within a single program. You can save time and memory by just entering the first two letters of a variable's name. You should still find the first two letters remind you what the variable name represents.

The first line in our next section clears the screen, before the following variables are initialized: STRENGTH, WEALTH, FOOD, TALLY, MK. If STRENGTH ever gets to zero, the game is over. WEALTH can be used to buy FOOD which can be eaten to restore STRENGTH. TALLY is a simple count of how long you have survived within the environment (one is added to TALLY each time you move) and MK is the count of monsters killed. These lines initialize the variables we've just discussed:

```
2610 CLS
2620 STRENGTH=100
2630 WEALTH=75
2640 FOOD=0
2650 TALLY=0
2660 MK=0:REM NO. OF MONSTERS KILLED
```

The Adventure is heightened if the computer uses the player's name from time to time, so line 2750 asks for the name, and allots N$ (for "Name string") to this. Line 2760 clears the screen of the question and answer, ready for the game itself to get underway.

The game begins outside the castle, in what we've designated "room 6," so the variable RO (for "ROom") is set equal to 6 in line 2770.

There are a number of things the player can manipulate or wear during the game, and the variable names to show possession of these are set to zero in lines 2780 to 2820. If any of these is changed to equal one, the player is carrying or wearing the object. This makes the purchase of, say, an axe very easy. If the variable AXE equals zero, the player does not have an axe. If AXE becomes equal to one, the computer can print out "YOU ARE CARRYING AN AXE." If the player drops the axe in a battle (as can happen in our second, more elaborate, version of WEREWOLVES AND WANDERER), this can be indicated simply by resetting the variable AXE to equal zero.

Here's the code to get the player's name, set the initial room value, and assign a value of zero to a number of variables:

```
2750 INPUT "WHAT IS YOUR NAME, EXPLORER"
;N$
```

```
2760 CLS
2770 RO=6:REM STARTING POSITION (RO=ROOM
 NUMBER)
2780 SWORD=0
2790 AMULET=0
2800 AXE=0
2810 SUIT=0
2820 LIGHT=0
```

From this chapter, you have learned how to place objects and entities within the Adventure program. As you can see, these add not only to the "reality" of the Adventure environment, but form part of the reasons why the Adventure is being undertaken. Who would risk multiple death, if precious gems were not the reward?

8

THE MAJOR HANDLING ROUTINE

It is time now to investigate the section of program which lies at the heart of the entire Adventure, the Major Handling Routine.

A Short Delay

Before we look at that, however, I want to show you a very short section of program, really only one line, which is very important to pacing the running of the program.

In contrast with many Adventure programs which allow a large vocabulary, and look at two or more words at a time, our WERE-WOLVES AND WANDERER only responds to a limited vocabulary. Because of this, it reacts very rapidly to input from the player. In many cases, this reaction is so fast there is not even time to read what is on the screen before it scrolls off.

Therefore, a delay loop has been included within the program, at line 3520. It runs from 1 to 900 at the moment, which seems ideal to me on the system on which the program was developed. However, you may like to add to, or subtract from, it for your computer.

Here's the delay loop:

```
3500 REM ******************
3510 REM ADJUST LOOP BELOW TO YOUR SYSTE
M
3520 FOR T=1 TO 900:NEXT T
3530 RETURN
```

You'll find this is called over and over again throughout the program, not only to give you a chance to read information on the screen before it vanishes, but to pace such things as a fight with a monster, or the descent of the elevator.

Your Strength Fades

The game is over if you run out of strength, as was pointed out earlier. Therefore, you have to keep an eye on your strength rating, which diminishes throughout the game. You replenish your strength by eating food, which you can buy with the proceeds of treasure you find lying around the castle.

Here's the first part of the Major Handling Routine, which subtracts five from your strength (variable name STRENGTH) each time you move:

```
150 REM ************************
160 REM MAJOR HANDLING ROUTINE
170 STRENGTH = STRENGTH - 5
180 IF STRENGTH<10 THEN PRINT "WARNING,
";N$;", YOUR STRENGTH":PRINT "IS RUNNING
 LOW":PRINT
190 IF STRENGTH < 1 THEN 2300:REM DEATH
```

As you can see, line 180 warns you that your strength is getting low if STRENGTH falls below 10. You will discover later that your strength can also fall during a fight. Sometimes you'll see this drops quite drastically if you are wounded.

If your strength falls below one (line 190), the program directs you to the Dead End subroutine from line 2290:

```
2290 REM ***************
2300 REM DEAD END
2310 PRINT "YOU HAVE DIED........"
2320 GOSUB 3520
2330 GOTO 120
```

When you construct your own programs, you'll discover that—within limits—the more things the player has to manage at a time, the more satisfying the program is to run. You should therefore aim to have something like our STRENGTH problem in your own programs, and a clear penalty, like our Dead End routine, if the problem is not handled satisfactorily.

The Final Reckoning

The final score in WEREWOLVES AND WANDERER is related—as was pointed out earlier—to a number of factors. One of these is TALLY, the time for which you manage to survive. Each time the program traverses the rocky ground of the Major Handling Routine, it runs through line 200, which increments your TALLY by one:

```
200 TALLY = TALLY + 1
```

At the very end of the program, whether you've managed to find the exit or not, your score will be added up. Your score is three times your TALLY, plus five times your STRENGTH, plus two times your WEALTH, plus the value of your uneaten FOOD and thirty times the number of monsters you have killed (variable name MK). It is evident that the number of monsters killed has more effect on your final score than just about any other item. Here's the section of code which works out your final score:

```
120 PRINT:PRINT "YOUR SCORE IS";
130 PRINT 3*TALLY + 5*STRENGTH + 2*WEALT
H + FOOD + 30*MK
140 END
```

There are is an infinite number of ways the final score can be calculated in an Adventure game. This is done by a simple scoring system in WEREWOLVES AND WANDERER, one you may well wish to modify. So long as your own games have some method of assessing the success or otherwise of a trek through your environment, it doesn't really matter what sort of final tallying system you devise. It can be as elaborate, or simple, as you choose.

Maintaining the Status Quo

As you saw in the sample run before we started outlining this program, the player gets a Status Report each time the program cycles through the Major Handling Routine.

The Status Report is handled by the lines from 210. Here is the first section of the Status Report program:

```
210 PRINT N$;", YOUR STRENGTH IS";STRENG
TH
```

```
220 IF WEALTH > 0 THEN PRINT "YOU HAVE $
";WEALTH
230 IF FOOD > 0 THEN PRINT "YOUR PROVISI
ONS SACK HOLDS";FOOD;"UNITS OF FOOD"
240 IF SUIT = 1 THEN PRINT "YOU ARE WEAR
ING ARMOR"
250 IF AXE=0 AND SWORD=0 AND AMULET=0 TH
EN 320
260 PRINT "YOU ARE CARRYING ";
270 IF AXE=1 THEN PRINT "AN AXE ";
280 IF SWORD=1 THEN PRINT "A SWORD ";
290 IF SWORD + AXE > 0 AND AMULET=1 THEN
 PRINT "AND ";
300 IF AMULET=1 THEN PRINT "THE MAGIC AM
ULET"
310 PRINT
```

Your name is used in line 210 (N$, for "name string") before you are told your STRENGTH and then WEALTH (line 220). If the variable FOOD is greater than zero (line 230) the computer knows you have bought some food which you have not yet eaten, and line 230 prints up a message to this effect. The same goes for the suit of armor (line 240), the axe (270), sword (280), and magic amulet (300). The other lines (those which print up such things as YOU ARE CARRYING and the word AND) also use the value of the variables AXE, SWORD, and AMULET to determine when these bridging words should be printed.

Let There Be Light

The presence, or otherwise, of a torch is crucial to many Adventure programs, including this one. The variable LIGHT is set initially to zero, meaning the player has not bought a "flaming torch."

If the player has no torch, he or she can see nothing. It is very dark within our castle. Lines 320 and 330 make up our Light/Dark Routine. If the player does not have a flaming torch (that is, variable LIGHT equals zero) the routine prints up IT IS TOO DARK TO SEE ANYTHING, and that's about it. If, however, you are carrying a torch (that is, LIGHT equals one) line 330 sends the computer to the vast subroutine from line 990 which describes what you can see in the room.

```
320 IF LIGHT=0 THEN PRINT "IT IS TOO DAR
K TO SEE ANYTHING"
```

```
330 IF LIGHT=1 THEN GOSUB 990:REM ROOM D
ESCRIPTION
```

Later on in the program, LIGHT is brought into play again. In the Pick Up Treasure Routine, the first line checks to see if you have a torch. If you do not, you are told curtly YOU CANNOT SEE WHERE IT IS, and are not given the chance to get it:

```
2370 IF LIGHT=0 THEN PRINT "YOU CANNOT S
EE WHERE IT IS":GOSUB 3520:RETURN
```

Objects in Disarray

You'll recall that the seventh element of a room held in the A array is set equal to the contents of the room. If this element is zero, there is nothing within the room the player can interact with.

The Object Handler depends totally upon this seventh element for its actions. Line 340 sets the variable K equal to the value of this element. Line 350 checks the value of K, knowing that if K equals zero, the room is effectively empty. If K is greater than nine (see line 360) the computer knows there is treasure in the room. If the room is not empty (K = 0) and does not contain treasure (K > 9) then the room must have a monster in it, and line 370 breaks the happy news.

```
340 K = A(RO,7):REM K IS SET TO CONTENTS
 OF ROOM
350 IF K=0 THEN 440:REM ROOM IS EMPTY
360 IF K>9 THEN PRINT "THERE IS TREASURE
 HERE WORTH $";K:GOTO 440
370 PRINT:PRINT:PRINT "DANGER...THERE IS
 A MONSTER HERE....":GOSUB 3520
```

If there is a monster in the room (that is, if K is less than 0) the string variables M$ (for "monster string") is assigned to the name of one of the monsters. The variable FF (for "ferocity factor") is also assigned. The higher the FF, the lower the chance you have of winning a battle against the relevant monster.

However, as you'll see when we look at The Battle later on, the weapons you hold, and whether or not you are wearing armor, can modify the ferocity factor in your favor.

The next section of the program (lines 380 through to 440) assign the monster's name to M$, the ferocity factor to FF, and tells you all about it.

```
380 IF K=-1 THEN M$="FEROCIOUS WEREWOLF"
:FF=5
390 IF K=-2 THEN M$="FANATICAL FLESHGORG
ER":FF=10
400 IF K=-3 THEN M$="MALOVENTY MALDEMER"
:FF=15
410 IF K=-4 THEN M$="DEVASTATING ICE-DRA
GON":FF=20
420 PRINT:PRINT "IT IS A ";M$
430 PRINT:PRINT "THE DANGER LEVEL IS";FF
;"!!"
440 GOSUB 3520
```

You can see how the "major handling routine" contributes another link in the chain which forges a feeling of reality in the Adventure environment. Any player action—such as picking up the torch—which produces a change within the Adventure, helps build mental images which sustain the illusion of the Adventure.

9

INTERPRETING YOUR COMMANDS

A Limited Vocabulary

WEREWOLVES AND WANDERER recognizes a strictly limited vocabulary. While this diminishes the realism of the Adventure to some extent (if such an arcane environment and such possibilities of interaction could ever be said to be "realistic"), it simplifies the construction of the program, and ensures that it runs as quickly as possible.

The program accepts your commands in lines 450 to 470, prompting you with WHAT DO YOU WANT TO DO?

You can enter the full word (such as NORTH) or just the first letter. As you can see, the last part of line 460 cuts the input down to a single letter anyway, so you may as well just enter the first letter of your command.

```
450 PRINT:PRINT:PRINT "WHAT DO YOU WANT
TO DO";
460 INPUT A$:A$=LEFT$(A$,1)
470 IF K<0 AND A$<>"F" AND A$<>"R" THEN
460
```

Here is the vocabulary the program recognizes:

N—NORTH S—SOUTH
E—EAST W—WEST
U—UP D—DOWN
F—FIGHT R—RUN
M—MAGIC (AMULET, used to trigger the amulet, which moves you to a room selected at random within the castle)
I—INVENTORY (to add to your possessions, and used if you want, for example, to buy food or an axe)
Q—QUIT (to terminate the Adventure at any time)
P—PICK UP (treasure)

Once you've entered your command, and it has been reduced (if necessary) to a single letter, the program draws a line across the screen to help organize the information on it.

If you have entered "Q" (for "quit"), the program goes straight to line 120 where your final score is calculated and printed:

```
480 PRINT:PRINT:PRINT "-----------------
-------------------":PRINT
490 IF A$="Q" THEN 120
```

As was explained much earlier in this book, the computer knows from the contents of the A array which directions are valid for travel from the current room. You'll see here that a different message is triggered for an attempt to move in each direction. This gives the impression that the computer is choosing from a vast set of possible replies, rather than just saying each time "YOU CAN'T GO THAT WAY."

```
500 IF A$="N" AND A(RO,1)=0 THEN PRINT "
NO EXIT THAT WAY":GOTO 440
510 IF A$="S" AND A(RO,2)=0 THEN PRINT "
THERE IS NO EXIT SOUTH":GOTO 440
520 IF A$="E" AND A(RO,3)=0 THEN PRINT "
YOU CANNOT GO IN THAT DIRECTION":GOTO 44
0
530 IF A$="W" AND A(RO,4)=0 THEN PRINT "
YOU CANNOT MOVE THROUGH SOLID STONE":GOT
O 440
540 IF A$="U" AND A(RO,5)=0 THEN PRINT "
THERE IS NO WAY UP FROM HERE":GOTO 440
```

```
550 IF A$="D" AND A(RO,6)=0 THEN PRINT "
YOU CANNOT DESCEND FROM HERE":GOTO 440
```

Fight or Flight

When confronted with a monster, you can enter either "F" (if you want to fight) or "R" (if you want to run). But, because we do not want to encourage cowardice, you'll discover that around 70% of the time you attempt to run, the computer will tell you it is impossible.

Line 560 is used to generate a random number between zero and one if the "R" option is entered, and if this random number is greater than .7, the program jumps to the Unsuccessful Attempt To Run routine:

```
560 IF A$="R" AND RND(1)>.7 THEN 2420
```

When it hits the routine, the computer tells you NO, YOU MUST STAND AND FIGHT and then changes your order to "F" and then returns to the field of action:

```
2410 REM ***************
2420 REM UNSUCCESSFUL ATTEMPT TO RUN
2430 PRINT "NO YOU MUST STAND AND FIGHT"

2440 A$="F"
2450 GOSUB 3520
2460 GOTO 590
```

If, however, the random number generated is not greater than .7, you are asked which direction you wish to run in:

```
570 IF A$="R" THEN PRINT "WHICH WAY DO Y
OU WANT TO FLEE";:GOTO 460
```

There is one more possibility. A player may enter "F" when there is no monster in the room. A badly written program may well then obligingly produce a monster out of nowhere. WEREWOLVES AND WANDERER gets around this by checking to see, when an "F" command has been entered, whether the vital seventh element is less than zero, and if it is not, points out THERE IS NOTHING TO FIGHT HERE and then goes back to 440 for a new command:

```
580 IF A$="F" AND A(RO,7)>-1 THEN PRINT
"THERE IS NOTHING TO FIGHT HERE":GOTO 44
0
```

You'll recall how, at the start of the book, I mentioned that some commercial Adventures, such as *Zork*, allow for whole sentences to be entered by the player. Our single-letter inputs seem pretty tame compared to this. But, as you'll see in our final program—CHATEAU GAILLARD—which accepts two-word commands, the way the program processes the single-letter input in this program forms the basis of the mechanism used for two, or more, word inputs.

10

SPEAKING IN OTHER TONGUES

Here's the routine which acts on the other possible inputs:

```
590 IF A$="I" THEN GOSUB 3010:RETURN
600 IF A$="C" AND FOOD=0 THEN PRINT "YOU
 HAVE NO FOOD":GOTO 440
610 IF A$="P" THEN GOSUB 2350:RETURN
620 IF A$="F" THEN 730
640 IF A$="C" THEN GOSUB 2480:RETURN
650 IF A$="N" THEN RO=A(RO,1)
660 IF A$="S" THEN RO=A(RO,2)
670 IF A$="E" THEN RO=A(RO,3)
680 IF A$="W" THEN RO=A(RO,4)
690 IF A$="U" THEN RO=A(RO,5)
700 IF A$="D" THEN RO=A(RO,6)
710 RETURN
```

You'll see (line 600) that if the player has entered "C" (for "consume," indicating a desire to eat), a check is made to see if there is any available food. If the variable FOOD equals zero, you are told YOU HAVE NO FOOD, and the computer returns to 440 for a new command.

The lines 650 through to 700 move you within the castle environment, as was explained earlier.

Making Magic

If you enter "M" (for "magic amulet") you'll be transported somewhere at random within the castle (but not to the entrance or exit). Only one line is needed to achieve this:

```
630 IF A$="M" THEN RO=INT(RND(1)*19)+1:I
F RO=6 OR RO=11 THEN 630 ELSE 710
```

If you enter a "C" (for "consume") you are sent to the Eat Food routine, from line 2470, where the computer first checks to see if you have any food. If you do not (that is, the variable FOOD equals zero) the program returns from the subroutine.

If you do have food, the computer tells you how much you have, and then you are asked how much you want to eat (line 2520). Each unit of food gives you five units of strength (line 2560). After a short delay (called by 2570) the program returns:

```
2470 REM ***************
2480 REM EAT FOOD
2490 CLS
2500 IF FOOD<1 THEN RETURN
2510 PRINT "YOU HAVE";FOOD;"UNITS OF FOO
D"
2520 PRINT "HOW MANY DO YOU WANT TO EAT"
;
2530 INPUT Z
2540 IF Z>FOOD THEN 2530
2550 FOOD=INT(FOOD-Z)
2560 STRENGTH=INT(STRENGTH+5*Z)
2570 GOSUB 3520:CLS
2580 RETURN
```

Picking Up Treasure

The Pick Up Treasure routine from 2340 has two checks which are imposed before you are able to actually take possession of treasure to add to your store of wealth.

First the program checks to see if there is actually any treasure there (line 2360), sending you back to enter a new command with the words THERE IS NO TREASURE TO PICK UP. Once you have passed this hurdle, the computer checks to see if you have a flaming torch. You'll recall we discussed this earlier, when looking at the Light/Dark Routine. Line 2370 was outlined at that time, and this is the line which makes the check.

If you have passed both of these checks, the value of the treasure is added to your wealth (line 2380) and the room is "emptied" (2390) by setting the relevant element to zero so that you cannot simply revisit the same room over and over again and pick up the same treasure several times.

```
2340 REM ***************
2350 REM PICK UP TREASURE
2360 IF A(RO,7)<10 THEN PRINT "THERE IS
NO TREASURE TO PICK UP":GOSUB 3520:RETUR
N
2380 WEALTH=WEALTH + A(RO,7)
2390 A(RO,7)=0
2400 RETURN
```

The Quartermaster's Store

One of your real tests within Adventure programs—after the major tests of trying to make sense of the environment, and staying alive—is the management of your resources. You'll recall I suggested that the more you expect the player to do on each game turn, the more satisfactory the program is likely to be.

Although you know, for example, that you need a torch in order to see anything, and to pick up treasure, a new player to the game may take quite a while to come to this conclusion. All a new player needs to know is the vocabulary, the fact that if he or she runs out of strength death is on the way, and that the purpose of the quest is to find the exit from the castle.

When you're designing an Adventure program, work out exactly what you're going to tell the player before the start of a game. An Adventure game with a computer is in part like an extended puzzle, in which the player tries to work out the problems set by the programmer. In WEREWOLVES AND WANDERER, as with the programs you are likely to write, there is far more happening than the simple solving of puzzles set by the programmer.

The Inventory/Provisions routine of this program is one of the keys to controlling the game. Once a player realizes that a torch is vital, and that it can be bought by going to the Inventory/Provisions routine, and that possession of an axe, sword or magic amulet can be a great help in trouble, he or she is well on the way to ensuring survival until the map of the castle can be deduced.

The Inventory/Provisions routine is largely self-explanatory. Here it is:

```
3000 REM ********************************
3010 REM INVENTORY/PROVISIONS
3020 PRINT "PROVISIONS & INVENTORY"
3030 GOSUB 3260
3040 IF WEALTH<.1 THEN Z=0:GOTO 3130
3050 PRINT "YOU CAN BUY 1 - FLAMING TORC
H ($15)"
3060 PRINT "                2 - AXE ($10)"
3070 PRINT "                3 - SWORD ($20)"
3080 PRINT "                4 - FOOD ($2 PER
 UNIT)"
3090 PRINT "                5 - MAGIC AMULET
 ($30)"
3100 PRINT "                6 - SUIT OF ARMO
R ($50)"
3110 PRINT "                0 - TO CONTINUE
ADVENTURE"
3120 INPUT "ENTER NO. OF ITEM REQUIRED";
Z
3130 IF Z=0 THEN CLS:RETURN
3140 IF Z=1 THEN LIGHT=1:WEALTH=WEALTH-1
5
3150 IF Z=2 THEN AXE=1:WEALTH=WEALTH-10
3160 IF Z=3 THEN SWORD=1:WEALTH=WEALTH-2
0
3170 IF Z=5 THEN AMULET=1:WEALTH=WEALTH-
30
3180 IF Z=6 THEN SUIT=1:WEALTH=WEALTH-50
3190 IF WEALTH<0 THEN PRINT "YOU HAVE TR
IED TO CHEAT ME!":WEALTH=0:SUIT=0:LIGHT=
0:AXE=0:SWORD=0:AMULET=0:FOOD=INT(FOOD/4
):GOSUB 3520
3200 IF Z<>4 THEN 3030
3210 INPUT "HOW MANY UNITS OF FOOD";Q:Q=
INT(Q)
3220 IF 2*Q>WEALTH THEN PRINT "YOU HAVEN
'T GOT ENOUGH MONEY":GOTO 3210
3230 FOOD=FOOD+Q
```

```
3240 WEALTH=WEALTH-2*Q
3250 GOTO 3030
3260 IF WEALTH>0 THEN PRINT:PRINT:PRINT
"YOU HAVE $";WEALTH
3270 IF WEALTH=0 THEN PRINT "YOU HAVE NO
 MONEY":GOSUB 3520:RETURN
3280 FOR J=1 TO 4:PRINT:NEXT J
3290 RETURN
```

You'll see the program first checks to see how much money you have (by going to the subroutine from 3260) and tells you the state of your finances. It will send you back to the main program (3040) if you have no money left (that is, if the variable WEALTH has a value less than .1).

Next the menu of possibilities is shown, with a code number next to each. You enter a 1 if you want to buy a flaming torch, for instance, 6 for a suit of armor, and 0 to return to the main program. After you enter your chosen number (3120) the computer uses the lines from 3130 through to 3180 to allow you to "make your purchase" by modifying variables and subtracting the cost from your WEALTH. This holds true except for FOOD (item 4 on the menu) which is handled slightly differently.

Do not, whatever you do, try to cheat by buying more than you can afford. The drastic line 3190 prints up YOU HAVE TRIED TO CHEAT ME and everything you own—except for one quarter of your food—is taken away for you.

If you have selected item 4 on the menu, indicating that you want to buy food, the routine from 3210 to 3240 looks after this for you.

The final subroutine (3260 to 3290) tells you how much money (if any) you have, PRINTs four blank lines, then returns for your next menu selection. This routine cycles—as I pointed out earlier—until you enter zero, indicating that you wish "TO CONTINUE ADVENTURE."

11

THE BIG FIGHT

Fights (or melees, as they are often known in Adventure games) are often the high points of a game. Do all you can to bring in the sound and graphics of your particular computer system to make the fights as exciting as possible.

Certainly, you should dress up the whole fight sequence in WEREWOLVES AND WANDERER and then go on to add similar effects to fight sequences you initiate in your own programs.

The fight consists of three distinct segments, and each segment should be handled as a separate programming task. The three segments, which we will discuss one at a time, are Preparation, The Battle itself, and The Result.

Be Prepared

The fight segment uses INKEY$ to get it underway. (You can, by the way, change nearly all player inputs in WEREWOLVES AND WANDERER into INKEY$ inputs.) Line 740 waits until you are not touching the keyboard, then prints up (750) the message PRESS ANY KEY TO FIGHT. Line 760 holds the action until a key is pressed.

Here's the Preparation segment of the program:

```
720 REM ****************************
730 REM FIGHT
740 IF INKEY$<>"" THEN 740
750 PRINT "PRESS ANY KEY TO FIGHT"
760 IF INKEY$="" THEN 760
770 IF SUIT=1 THEN PRINT "YOUR ARMOR INC
```

```
REASES YOUR CHANCE OF SUCCESS":FF=3*(INT
(FF/4)):GOSUB 3520
780 CLS:FOR J=1 TO 6:PRINT "*_*_*_*_*_
*_*_*_*_*_*_*_*_*_*_*_*_*_*":NEXT J
790 IF AXE=0 AND SWORD=0 THEN PRINT "YOU
 HAVE NO WEAPONS":PRINT "YOU MUST FIGHT
WITH BARE HANDS":FF=INT(FF + FF/5):GOTO
870
800 IF AXE=1 AND SWORD=0 THEN PRINT "YOU
 HAVE ONLY AN AXE TO FIGHT WITH":FF=4*IN
T(FF/5):GOTO 870
810 IF AXE=0 AND SWORD=1 THEN PRINT "YOU
 MUST FIGHT WITH YOUR SWORD":FF=3*INT(FF
/4):GOTO 870
820 INPUT "WHICH WEAPON? 1 - AXE, 2 - SW
ORD";Z
830 IF Z<1 OR Z>2 THEN 820
840 IF Z=1 THEN FF=4*INT(FF/5)
850 IF Z=2 THEN FF=3*INT(FF/4)
```

You'll recall from our talk about monsters that the variable FF stands for ferocity factor, and the higher the FF, the lower is your chance of defeating the particular monster. If you are wearing armor (as line 770 informs you) your chance of success is increased, because FF is set to three-quarters of its former value.

If you have no weapons (that is, AXE equals zero and SWORD equals zero), the FF is increased by one fifth. It is important in programs like this one to give the player a real reason for spending his or her hard-won wealth on things such as weaponry. Adjusting the chance of success—as fiddling with FF does in this program—gives a specific, and rational, reason to invest in weapons.

If you have both an axe and a sword, lines 820 and 830 allow you to choose from between them, modifying your chances accordingly.

Taking Up Arms

The Battle itself is controlled by lines 880 to 940:

```
860 REM **************************
870 REM THE BATTLE
880 PRINT:PRINT
890 IF RND(1)>.5 THEN PRINT M$;" ATTACKS
" ELSE PRINT "YOU ATTACK"
```

```
900 GOSUB 3520
910 IF RND(1)>.5 THEN PRINT:PRINT "YOU M
ANAGE TO WOUND IT":FF=INT(5*FF/6)
920 GOSUB 3520
930 IF RND(1)>.5 THEN PRINT:PRINT "THE M
ONSTER WOUNDS YOU!":STRENGTH=STRENGTH-5
940 IF RND(1)>.35 THEN 890
```

This routine actually "stage-manages" the fight, maintains a role as referee, and reports to you during the fight on how it is going. Each time you manage to wound the monster (line 910) the ferocity factor is reduced to five-sixths of its former value. Your strength is diminished by five each time the monster manages to wound you. Two-thirds of the time the computer comes to line 940, it will go back to line 890 for another round.

The Tumult and the Shouting Dies

Line 950 compares a number generated at random between zero and 15 with the ferocity factor, and if it is higher, gives you the victory, adding one to your MK (Monster Kill count). If you do not win, line 960 tells you the bad news, and halves your remaining strength.

```
950 IF RND(1)*16>FF THEN PRINT:PRINT "AN
D YOU MANAGED TO KILL THE ";M$:MK=MK+1:G
OTO 970
960 PRINT:PRINT "THE ";M$;" DEFEATED YOU
":STRENGTH=INT(STRENGTH/2)
970 A(RO,7)=0:GOSUB 3510:PRINT:PRINT:GOS
UB 3520:RETURN
```

The last line of this section gets rid of the monster, and after a pause, prints a few blank lines and another pause, sends you back to the main section of the program.

As I said at the beginning of this chapter, the melee is one area in Adventure programs when any effects that you can call into play are welcome. You should get some ideas on ways of dressing up fight sequences when I present an elaborated version of this program later on in the book, but you're sure to be able to work out many others for yourself, once you see the kind of things which can be done.

12

PEEKING INTO THE ROOMS

Room Descriptions

Room descriptions add a third dimension to the raw plans of your Adventure environment. You can add as many details as you like to describing each room or cavern your Adventurer discovers, or you can keep the descriptions short, and leave it up to the player's imagination to fill in the gaps.

I prefer to steer a middle course, adding some description, but not too much, to trigger the player's imagination but not to stifle it.

This section of the program is pretty simple to understand. The long ON GOSUB line (1010) sends the computer to the relevant room, printing up a brief description of the room, and pointing out where the windows and doors are.

You should now refer back to the maps of the various floors, and see how they relate to the descriptions given below:

```
980 REM ******************
990 REM ROOM DESCRIPTIONS
1000 PRINT:PRINT "************************
********":PRINT:PRINT
1010 ON RO GOSUB 1040,1100,1170,1230,128
0,1360,1410,1470,1540,1620,1700,1730,179
0,1860,1960,2030,2100,2160,2230
1020 RETURN
1030 REM *************
```

```
1040 REM ROOM 1
1050 PRINT "YOU ARE IN THE HALLWAY"
1060 PRINT "THERE IS A DOOR TO THE SOUTH
"
1070 PRINT "THROUGH WINDOWS TO THE NORTH
 YOU CAN SEE A SECRET HERB GARDEN"
1080 RETURN
1090 REM ************
1100 REM ROOM 2
1110 PRINT "THIS IS THE AUDIENCE CHAMBER
"
1120 PRINT "THERE IS A WINDOW TO THE WES
T. BY LOOKING TO THE RIGHT"
1130 PRINT "THROUGH IT YOU CAN SEE THE E
NTRANCE TO THE CASTLE."
1140 PRINT "DOORS LEAVE THIS ROOM TO THE
 NORTH, EAST AND SOUTH"
1150 RETURN
1160 REM ************
1170 REM ROOM 3
1180 PRINT "YOU ARE IN THE GREAT HALL, A
N L-SHAPED ROOM"
1190 PRINT "THERE ARE DOORS TO THE EAST
AND TO THE NORTH"
1200 PRINT "IN THE ALCOVE IS A DOOR TO T
HE WEST"
1210 RETURN
1220 REM ************
1230 REM ROOM 4
1240 PRINT "THIS IS THE MONARCH'S PRIVAT
E MEETING ROOM"
1250 PRINT "THERE IS A SINGLE EXIT TO TH
E SOUTH"
1260 RETURN
1270 REM ************
1280 REM ROOM 5
1290 PRINT "THIS INNER HALLWAY CONTAINS
A DOOR TO THE NORTH,"
1300 PRINT "AND ONE TO THE WEST, AND A C
IRCULAR STAIRWELL"
1310 PRINT "PASSES THROUGH THE ROOM"
1320 PRINT "YOU CAN SEE AN ORNAMENTAL LA
KE THROUGH THE"
1330 PRINT "WINDOWS TO THE SOUTH"
```

```
1340 RETURN
1350 REM ************
1360 REM ROOM 6
1370 PRINT "YOU ARE AT THE ENTRANCE TO A
 FORBIDDING-LOOKING"
1380 PRINT "STONE CASTLE.  YOU ARE FACIN
G EAST"
1390 RETURN
1400 REM ************
1410 REM ROOM 7
1420 PRINT "THIS IS THE CASTLE'S KITCHEN
. THROUGH WINDOWS IN"
1430 PRINT "THE NORTH WALL YOU CAN SEE A
 SECRET HERB GARDEN."
1440 PRINT "A DOOR LEAVES THE KITCHEN TO
 THE SOUTH"
1450 RETURN
1460 REM **************
1470 REM ROOM 8
1480 PRINT "YOU ARE IN THE STORE ROOM, A
MIDST SPICES,"
1490 PRINT "VEGETABLES, AND VAST SACKS O
F FLOUR AND"
1500 PRINT "OTHER PROVISIONS. THERE IS A
 DOOR TO THE NORTH"
1510 PRINT "AND ONE TO THE SOUTH"
1520 RETURN
1610 REM *************************
1620 REM ROOM 10
1630 PRINT "YOU ARE IN THE REAR VESTIBUL
E"
1640 PRINT "THERE ARE WINDOWS TO THE SOU
TH FROM WHICH"
1650 PRINT "YOU CAN SEE THE ORNAMENTAL L
AKE"
1660 PRINT "THERE IS AN EXIT TO THE EAST
, AND"
1670 PRINT "ONE TO THE NORTH"
1680 RETURN
1720 REM ***************
1730 REM ROOM 12
1740 PRINT "YOU ARE IN THE DANK, DARK DU
NGEON"
1750 PRINT "THERE IS A SINGLE EXIT, A SM
```

```
ALL HOLE IN"
1760 PRINT "WALL TOWARDS THE WEST"
1770 RETURN
1780 REM *****************
1790 REM ROOM 13
1800 PRINT "YOU ARE IN THE PRISON GUARDR
OOM, IN THE"
1810 PRINT "BASEMENT OF THE CASTLE. THE
STAIRWELL"
1820 PRINT "ENDS IN THIS ROOM. THERE IS
ONE OTHER"
1830 PRINT "EXIT, A SMALL HOLE IN THE EA
ST WALL"
1840 RETURN
1850 REM *****************
1860 REM ROOM 14
1870 PRINT "YOU ARE IN THE MASTER BEDROO
M ON THE UPPER"
1880 PRINT "LEVEL OF THE CASTLE...."
1890 PRINT "LOOKING DOWN FROM THE WINDOW
 TO THE WEST YOU"
1900 PRINT "CAN SEE THE ENTRANCE TO THE
CASTLE, WHILE THE"
1910 PRINT "SECRET HERB GARDEN IS VISIBL
E BELOW THE NORTH"
1920 PRINT "WINDOW. THERE ARE DOORS TO T
HE EAST AND"
1930 PRINT "TO THE SOUTH...."
1940 RETURN
1950 REM ****************
1960 REM ROOM 15
1970 PRINT "THIS IS THE L-SHAPED UPPER
HALLWAY."
1980 PRINT "TO THE NORTH IS A DOOR, AND
THERE IS A"
1990 PRINT "STAIRWELL IN THE HALL AS WEL
L. YOU CAN SEE"
2000 PRINT "THE LAKE THROUGH THE SOUTH W
INDOWS"
2010 RETURN
2020 REM *****************
2030 REM ROOM 16
2040 PRINT "THIS ROOM WAS USED AS THE CA
STLE TREASURY IN"
```

```
2050 PRINT "BY-GONE YEARS...."
2060 PRINT "THERE ARE NO WINDOWS, JUST E
XITS TO THE"
2070 PRINT "NORTH AND TO THE EAST"
2080 RETURN
2090 REM ***************
2100 REM ROOM 17
2110 PRINT "OOOOH...YOU ARE IN THE CHAMB
ERMAIDS' BEDROOM"
2120 PRINT "THERE IS AN EXIT TO THE WEST
 AND A DOOR"
2130 PRINT "TO THE SOUTH...."
2140 RETURN
2150 REM ****************
2160 REM ROOM 18
2170 PRINT "THIS TINY ROOM ON THE UPPER
LEVEL IS THE"
2180 PRINT "DRESSING CHAMBER. THERE IS A
 WINDOW TO THE"
2190 PRINT "NORTH, WITH A VIEW OF THE HE
RB GARDEN DOWN"
2200 PRINT "BELOW. A DOOR LEAVES TO THE
SOUTH"
2210 RETURN
2220 REM **************
2230 REM ROOM 19
2240 PRINT "THIS IS THE SMALL ROOM OUTSI
DE THE CASTLE"
2250 PRINT "LIFT WHICH CAN BE ENTERED BY
 A DOOR TO THE NORTH"
2260 PRINT "ANOTHER DOOR LEADS TO THE WE
ST. YOU CAN SEE"
2270 PRINT "THE LAKE THROUGH THE SOUTHER
N WINDOWS"
2280 RETURN
```

All these subroutines simply print out a description, then return to line 1020 which returns action to the main program.

Special Handling

Two rooms are different. Room 9 is, as you can see from the map, the elevator, and this needs special handling. The delay loop is called twice, and then RO is set to 10 (line 1590), the room you end up in after using the elevator, before the program returns to the main handler.

```
1530 REM ***************
1540 REM ROOM 9
1550 PRINT "YOU HAVE ENTERED THE LIFT...
"
1560 GOSUB 3520
1570 PRINT "IT SLOWLY DESCENDS..."
1580 GOSUB 3520
1590 RO=10
1600 GOTO 1000
```

The other room needing special handling is room 11, the final exit. When the computer comes to the relevant subroutine, it immediately hits a return. It is put here, within the other room subroutines, just to keep the program clear.

```
1690 REM ******************
1700 REM ROOM 11
1710 RETURN
```

Once you've made it to room 11, the program stops cycling, and then announces your success:

```
50 PRINT:PRINT "YOU'VE DONE IT!!":GOSUB
3520:PRINT "THAT WAS THE EXIT FROM THE C
ASTLE"
60 GOSUB 3520
70 PRINT:PRINT "YOU HAVE SUCCEEDED, ";N$
;"!"
80 PRINT:PRINT "YOU MANAGED TO GET OUT O
F THE CASTLE"
90 GOSUB 3520
100 PRINT:PRINT "WELL DONE!"
110 GOSUB 3520
```

From here it simply follows on to lines 120 and 130, which we discussed earlier, to print up your score, and end the game.

The examples given in this chapter should help you develop a number of ideas of your own to incorporate into room descriptions and "special events." CHATEAU GAILLARD, the final program in the book, includes some quite difficult "special handling" situations. Although these situations are a little more complex than those outlined in this chapter, they use the ideas we have discussed here. Therefore, it's probably a good idea to review and make sure you understand the material in this chapter before continuing.

13

WEREWOLVES AND WANDERER

I hope you've been entering the program section by section as you've come to it. This is the best way to learn the things I've included in the Adventure, and to determine for yourself how you can apply these ideas to your own Adventure programs.

Here now, is the complete listing of the program, in one run, so you can check the program you have entered section by section into your computer.

```
10 REM WEREWOLVES AND WANDERER
20 GOSUB 2600:REM INITIALISE
30 GOSUB 160
40 IF RO <> 11 THEN 30
50 PRINT:PRINT "YOU'VE DONE IT!!":GOSUB
3520:PRINT "THAT WAS THE EXIT FROM THE C
ASTLE"
60 GOSUB 3520
70 PRINT:PRINT "YOU HAVE SUCCEEDED, ";N$
;"!"
80 PRINT:PRINT "YOU MANAGED TO GET OUT O
F THE CASTLE"
90 GOSUB 3520
100 PRINT:PRINT "WELL DONE!"
110 GOSUB 3520
120 PRINT:PRINT "YOUR SCORE IS";
130 PRINT 3*TALLY + 5*STRENGTH + 2*WEALT
H + FOOD + 30*MK
```

```
140 END
150 REM ***********************
160 REM MAJOR HANDLING ROUTINE
170 STRENGTH = STRENGTH - 5
180 IF STRENGTH<10 THEN PRINT "WARNING,
";N$;", YOUR STRENGTH":PRINT "IS RUNNING
 LOW":PRINT
190 IF STRENGTH < 1 THEN 2300:REM DEATH
200 TALLY = TALLY + 1
210 PRINT N$;", YOUR STRENGTH IS";STRENG
TH
220 IF WEALTH > 0 THEN PRINT "YOU HAVE $
";WEALTH
230 IF FOOD > 0 THEN PRINT "YOUR PROVISI
ONS SACK HOLDS";FOOD;"UNITS OF FOOD"
240 IF SUIT = 1 THEN PRINT "YOU ARE WEAR
ING ARMOR"
250 IF AXE=0 AND SWORD=0 AND AMULET=0 TH
EN 320
260 PRINT "YOU ARE CARRYING ";
270 IF AXE=1 THEN PRINT "AN AXE ";
280 IF SWORD=1 THEN PRINT "A SWORD ";
290 IF SWORD + AXE > 0 AND AMULET=1 THEN
 PRINT "AND ";
300 IF AMULET=1 THEN PRINT "THE MAGIC AM
ULET"
310 PRINT
320 IF LIGHT=0 THEN PRINT "IT IS TOO DAR
K TO SEE ANYTHING"
330 IF LIGHT=1 THEN GOSUB 990:REM ROOM D
ESCRIPTION
340 K = A(RO,7):REM K IS SET TO CONTENTS
 OF ROOM
350 IF K=0 THEN 440:REM ROOM IS EMPTY
360 IF K>9 THEN PRINT "THERE IS TREASURE
 HERE WORTH $";K:GOTO 440
370 PRINT:PRINT:PRINT "DANGER...THERE IS
 A MONSTER HERE....":GOSUB 3520
380 IF K=-1 THEN M$="FEROCIOUS WEREWOLF"
:FF=5
390 IF K=-2 THEN M$="FANATICAL FLESHGORG
ER":FF=10
400 IF K=-3 THEN M$="MALOVENTY MALDEMER"
:FF=15
```

```
410 IF K=-4 THEN M$="DEVASTATING ICE-DRA
GON":FF=20
420 PRINT:PRINT "IT IS A ";M$
430 PRINT:PRINT "THE DANGER LEVEL IS";FF
;"!!"
440 GOSUB 3520
450 PRINT:PRINT:PRINT "WHAT DO YOU WANT
TO DO";
460 INPUT A$:A$=LEFT$(A$,1)
470 IF K<0 AND A$<>"F" AND A$<>"R" THEN
460
480 PRINT:PRINT:PRINT "-----------------
-------------------":PRINT
490 IF A$="Q" THEN 120
500 IF A$="N" AND A(RO,1)=0 THEN PRINT "
NO EXIT THAT WAY":GOTO 440
510 IF A$="S" AND A(RO,2)=0 THEN PRINT "
THERE IS NO EXIT SOUTH":GOTO 440
520 IF A$="E" AND A(RO,3)=0 THEN PRINT "
YOU CANNOT GO IN THAT DIRECTION":GOTO 44
0
530 IF A$="W" AND A(RO,4)=0 THEN PRINT "
YOU CANNOT MOVE THROUGH SOLID STONE":GOT
O 440
540 IF A$="U" AND A(RO,5)=0 THEN PRINT "
THERE IS NO WAY UP FROM HERE":GOTO 440
550 IF A$="D" AND A(RO,6)=0 THEN PRINT "
YOU CANNOT DESCEND FROM HERE":GOTO 440
560 IF A$="R" AND RND(1)>.7 THEN 2420
570 IF A$="R" THEN PRINT "WHICH WAY DO Y
OU WANT TO FLEE";:GOTO 460
580 IF A$="F" AND A(RO,7)>-1 THEN PRINT
"THERE IS NOTHING TO FIGHT HERE":GOTO 44
0
590 IF A$="I" THEN GOSUB 3010:RETURN
600 IF A$="C" AND FOOD=0 THEN PRINT "YOU
 HAVE NO FOOD":GOTO 440
610 IF A$="P" THEN GOSUB 2350:RETURN
620 IF A$="F" THEN 730
630 IF A$="M" THEN RO=INT(RND(1)*19)+1:I
F RO=6 OR RO=11 THEN 630 ELSE 710
640 IF A$="C" THEN GOSUB 2480:RETURN
650 IF A$="N" THEN RO=A(RO,1)
660 IF A$="S" THEN RO=A(RO,2)
```

```
670 IF A$="E" THEN RO=A(RO,3)
680 IF A$="W" THEN RO=A(RO,4)
690 IF A$="U" THEN RO=A(RO,5)
700 IF A$="D" THEN RO=A(RO,6)
710 RETURN
720 REM ***************************
730 REM FIGHT
740 IF INKEY$<>"" THEN 740
750 PRINT "PRESS ANY KEY TO FIGHT"
760 IF INKEY$="" THEN 760
770 IF SUIT=1 THEN PRINT "YOUR ARMOR INC
REASES YOUR CHANCE OF SUCCESS":FF=3*(INT
(FF/4)):GOSUB 3520
780 CLS:FOR J=1 TO 6:PRINT "*_*_*_*_*_
*_*_*_*_*_*_*_*_*_*_*_*_*_*":NEXT J
790 IF AXE=0 AND SWORD=0 THEN PRINT "YOU
 HAVE NO WEAPONS":PRINT "YOU MUST FIGHT
WITH BARE HANDS":FF=INT(FF + FF/5):GOTO
870
800 IF AXE=1 AND SWORD=0 THEN PRINT "YOU
 HAVE ONLY AN AXE TO FIGHT WITH":FF=4*IN
T(FF/5):GOTO 870
810 IF AXE=0 AND SWORD=1 THEN PRINT "YOU
 MUST FIGHT WITH YOUR SWORD":FF=3*INT(FF
/4):GOTO 870
820 INPUT "WHICH WEAPON? 1 - AXE, 2 - SW
ORD";Z
830 IF Z<1 OR Z>2 THEN 820
840 IF Z=1 THEN FF=4*INT(FF/5)
850 IF Z=2 THEN FF=3*INT(FF/4)
860 REM ***************************
870 REM THE BATTLE
880 PRINT:PRINT
890 IF RND(1)>.5 THEN PRINT M$;" ATTACKS
" ELSE PRINT "YOU ATTACK"
900 GOSUB 3520
910 IF RND(1)>.5 THEN PRINT:PRINT "YOU M
ANAGE TO WOUND IT":FF=INT(5*FF/6)
920 GOSUB 3520
930 IF RND(1)>.5 THEN PRINT:PRINT "THE M
ONSTER WOUNDS YOU!":STRENGTH=STRENGTH-5
940 IF RND(1)>.35 THEN 890
950 IF RND(1)*16>FF THEN PRINT:PRINT "AN
D YOU MANAGED TO KILL THE ";M$:MK=MK+1:
```

```
GOTO 970
960 PRINT:PRINT "THE ";M$;" DEFEATED YOU
":STRENGTH=INT(STRENGTH/2)
970 A(RO,7)=0:GOSUB 3410:PRINT:PRINT:GOS
UB 3520:RETURN
980 REM *****************
990 REM ROOM DESCRIPTIONS
1000 PRINT:PRINT "**********************
********":PRINT:PRINT
1010 ON RO GOSUB 1040,1100,1170,1230,128
0,1360,1410,1470,1540,1620,1700,1730,179
0,1860,1960,2030,2100,2160,2230
1020 RETURN
1030 REM ************
1040 REM ROOM 1
1050 PRINT "YOU ARE IN THE HALLWAY"
1060 PRINT "THERE IS A DOOR TO THE SOUTH
"
1070 PRINT "THROUGH WINDOWS TO THE NORTH
 YOU CAN SEE A SECRET HERB GARDEN"
1080 RETURN
1090 REM ************
1100 REM ROOM 2
1110 PRINT "THIS IS THE AUDIENCE CHAMBER
"
1120 PRINT "THERE IS A WINDOW TO THE WES
T. BY LOOKING TO THE RIGHT"
1130 PRINT "THROUGH IT YOU CAN SEE THE E
NTRANCE TO THE CASTLE."
1140 PRINT "DOORS LEAVE THIS ROOM TO THE
 NORTH, EAST AND SOUTH"
1150 RETURN
1160 REM ************
1170 REM ROOM 3
1180 PRINT "YOU ARE IN THE GREAT HALL, A
N L-SHAPED ROOM"
1190 PRINT "THERE ARE DOORS TO THE EAST
AND TO THE NORTH"
1200 PRINT "IN THE ALCOVE IS A DOOR TO T
HE WEST"
1210 RETURN
1220 REM ************
1230 REM ROOM 4
1240 PRINT "THIS IS THE MONARCH'S PRIVAT
```

```
E MEETING ROOM"
1250 PRINT "THERE IS A SINGLE EXIT TO TH
E SOUTH"
1260 RETURN
1270 REM *************
1280 REM ROOM 5
1290 PRINT "THIS INNER HALLWAY CONTAINS
A DOOR TO THE NORTH,"
1300 PRINT "AND ONE TO THE WEST, AND A C
IRCULAR STAIRWELL"
1310 PRINT "PASSES THROUGH THE ROOM"
1320 PRINT "YOU CAN SEE AN ORNAMENTAL LA
KE THROUGH THE"
1330 PRINT "WINDOWS TO THE SOUTH"
1340 RETURN
1350 REM *************
1360 REM ROOM 6
1370 PRINT "YOU ARE AT THE ENTRANCE TO A
 FORBIDDING-LOOKING"
1380 PRINT "STONE CASTLE.  YOU ARE FACIN
G EAST"
1390 RETURN
1400 REM *************
1410 REM ROOM 7
1420 PRINT "THIS IS THE CASTLE'S KITCHEN
. THROUGH WINDOWS IN"
1430 PRINT "THE NORTH WALL YOU CAN SEE A
 SECRET HERB GARDEN."
1440 PRINT "A DOOR LEAVES THE KITCHEN TO
 THE SOUTH"
1450 RETURN
1460 REM ***************
1470 REM ROOM 8
1480 PRINT "YOU ARE IN THE STORE ROOM, A
MIDST SPICES,"
1490 PRINT "VEGETABLES, AND VAST SACKS O
F FLOUR AND"
1500 PRINT "OTHER PROVISIONS. THERE IS A
 DOOR TO THE NORTH"
1510 PRINT "AND ONE TO THE SOUTH"
1520 RETURN
1530 REM ***************
1540 REM ROOM 9
1550 PRINT "YOU HAVE ENTERED THE LIFT..."
```

```
1560 GOSUB 3520
1570 PRINT "IT SLOWLY DESCENDS..."
1580 GOSUB 3520
1590 RO=10
1600 GOTO 1000
1610 REM ***************************
1620 REM ROOM 10
1630 PRINT "YOU ARE IN THE REAR VESTIBUL
E"
1640 PRINT "THERE ARE WINDOWS TO THE SOU
TH FROM WHICH YOU"
1650 PRINT "YOU CAN SEE THE ORNAMENTAL L
AKE"
1660 PRINT "THERE IS AN EXIT TO THE EAST
, AND"
1670 PRINT "ONE TO THE NORTH"
1680 RETURN
1690 REM ******************
1700 REM ROOM 11
1710 RETURN
1720 REM *****************
1730 REM ROOM 12
1740 PRINT "YOU ARE IN THE DANK, DARK DU
NGEON"
1750 PRINT "THERE IS A SINGLE EXIT, A SM
ALL HOLE IN"
1760 PRINT "WALL TOWARDS THE WEST"
1770 RETURN
1780 REM *****************
1790 REM ROOM 13
1800 PRINT "YOU ARE IN THE PRISON GUARDR
OOM, IN THE"
1810 PRINT "BASEMENT OF THE CASTLE. THE
STAIRWELL"
1820 PRINT "ENDS IN THIS ROOM. THERE IS
ONE OTHER"
1830 PRINT "EXIT, A SMALL HOLE IN THE EA
ST WALL"
1840 RETURN
1850 REM *****************
1860 REM ROOM 14
1870 PRINT "YOU ARE IN THE MASTER BEDROO
M ON THE UPPER"
1880 PRINT "LEVEL OF THE CASTLE...."
```

```
1890 PRINT "LOOKING DOWN FROM THE WINDOW
 TO THE WEST YOU"
1900 PRINT "CAN SEE THE ENTRANCE TO THE
CASTLE, WHILE THE"
1910 PRINT "SECRET HERB GARDEN IS VISIBL
E BELOW THE NORTH"
1920 PRINT "WINDOW. THERE ARE DOORS TO T
HE EAST AND"
1930 PRINT "TO THE SOUTH...."
1940 RETURN
1950 REM ***************
1960 REM ROOM 15
1970 PRINT "THIS IS THE L-SHAPPED UPPER
HALLWAY."
1980 PRINT "TO THE NORTH IS A DOOR, AND
THERE IS A"
1990 PRINT "STAIRWELL IN THE HALL AS WEL
L. YOU CAN SEE"
2000 PRINT "THE LAKE THROUGH THE SOUTH W
INDOWS"
2010 RETURN
2020 REM ****************
2030 REM ROOM 16
2040 PRINT "THIS ROOM WAS USED AS THE CA
STLE TREASURY IN"
2050 PRINT "BY-GONE YEARS...."
2060 PRINT "THERE ARE NO WINDOWS, JUST E
XITS TO THE"
2070 PRINT "NORTH AND TO THE EAST"
2080 RETURN
2090 REM **************
2100 REM ROOM 17
2110 PRINT "OOOOH...YOU ARE IN THE CHAMB
ERMAIDS' BEDROOM"
2120 PRINT "THERE IS AN EXIT TO THE WEST
 AND A DOOR"
2130 PRINT "TO THE SOUTH...."
2140 RETURN
2150 REM ***************
2160 REM ROOM 18
2170 PRINT "THIS TINY ROOM ON THE UPPER
LEVEL IS THE"
2180 PRINT "DRESSING CHAMBER. THERE IS A
 WINDOW TO THE"
```

```
2190 PRINT "NORTH, WITH A VIEW OF THE HE
RB GARDEN DOWN"
2200 PRINT "BELOW. A DOOR LEAVES TO THE
SOUTH"
2210 RETURN
2220 REM **************
2230 REM ROOM 19
2240 PRINT "THIS IS THE SMALL ROOM OUTSI
DE THE CASTLE"
2250 PRINT "LIFT WHICH CAN BE ENTERED BY
 A DOOR TO THE NORTH"
2260 PRINT "ANOTHER DOOR LEADS TO THE WE
ST. YOU CAN SEE"
2270 PRINT "THE LAKE THROUGH THE SOUTHER
N WINDOWS"
2280 RETURN
2290 REM ***************
2300 REM DEAD END
2310 PRINT "YOU HAVE DIED........"
2320 GOSUB 3520
2330 GOTO 120
2340 REM ***************
2350 REM PICK UP TREASURE
2360 IF A(RO,7)<10 THEN PRINT "THERE IS
NO TREASURE TO PICK UP":GOSUB 3520:RETUR
N
2370 IF LIGHT=0 THEN PRINT "YOU CANNOT S
EE WHERE IT IS":GOSUB 3520:RETURN
2380 WEALTH=WEALTH + A(RO,7)
2390 A(RO,7)=0
2400 RETURN
2410 REM ***************
2420 REM UNSUCCESSFUL ATTEMPT TO RUN
2430 PRINT "NO YOU MUST STAND AND FIGHT"

2440 A$="F"
2450 GOSUB 3520
2460 GOTO 590
2470 REM ***************
2480 REM EAT FOOD
2490 CLS
2500 IF FOOD<1 THEN RETURN
2510 PRINT "YOU HAVE";FOOD;"UNITS OF FOO
D"
```

```
2520 PRINT "HOW MANY DO YOU WANT TO EAT"
;
2530 INPUT Z
2540 IF Z>FOOD THEN 2530
2550 FOOD=INT(FOOD-Z)
2560 STRENGTH=INT(STRENGTH+5*Z)
2570 GOSUB 3410:CLS
2580 RETURN
2590 REM ************
2600 REM INITIALISE
2610 CLS
2620 STRENGTH=100
2630 WEALTH=75
2640 FOOD=0
2650 TALLY=0
2660 MK=0:REM NO. OF MONSTERS KILLED
2670 REM ***************
2680 REM SET UP CASTLE

2690 DIM A(19,7)
2700 FOR B=1 TO 19
2710 FOR C=1 TO 7
2720 READ A(B,C)
2730 NEXT C
2740 NEXT B
2750 INPUT "WHAT IS YOUR NAME, EXPLORER"
;N$
2760 CLS
2770 RO=6:REM STARTING POSITION (RO=ROOM
 NUMBER)
2780 SWORD=0
2790 AMULET=0
2800 AXE=0
2810 SUIT=0
2820 LIGHT=0
2830 REM ***************
2840 REM ALLOT TREASURE
2850 FOR J = 1 TO 4
2860 M=INT(RND(1)*19)+1
2870 IF M=6 OR M=11 OR A(M,7)<>0 THEN 28
60
2880 A(M,7)=INT(RND(1)*100)+10
2890 NEXT J
2900 REM ***************
```

```
2910 REM ALLOT MONSTERS
2920 FOR J = 1 TO 4
2930 M=INT(RND(1)*18)+1
2940 IF M=6 OR M=11 OR A(M,7)<>0 THEN 29
30
2950 A(M,7)= -J
2960 NEXT J
2970 A(4,7)=100+INT(RND(1)*100)
2980 A(16,7)=100+INT(RND(1)*100)
2990 RETURN
3000 REM ******************************
3010 REM INVENTORY/PROVISIONS
3020 PRINT "PROVISIONS & INVENTORY"
3030 GOSUB 3260
3040 IF WEALTH<.1 THEN Z=0:GOTO 3130
3050 PRINT "YOU CAN BUY 1 - FLAMING TORC
H ($15)"
3060 PRINT "            2 - AXE ($10)"
3070 PRINT "            3 - SWORD ($20)"

3080 PRINT "            4 - FOOD ($2 PER
 UNIT)"
3090 PRINT "            5 - MAGIC AMULET
 ($30)"
3100 PRINT "            6 - SUIT OF ARMO
R ($50)"
3110 PRINT "            0 - TO CONTINUE
ADVENTURE"
3120 INPUT "ENTER NO. OF ITEM REQUIRED";
Z
3130 IF Z=0 THEN CLS:RETURN
3140 IF Z=1 THEN LIGHT=1:WEALTH=WEALTH-1
5
3150 IF Z=2 THEN AXE=1:WEALTH=WEALTH-10
3160 IF Z=3 THEN SWORD=1:WEALTH=WEALTH-2
0
3170 IF Z=5 THEN AMULET=1:WEALTH=WEALTH-
30
3180 IF Z=6 THEN SUIT=1:WEALTH=WEALTH-50

3190 IF WEALTH<0 THEN PRINT "YOU HAVE TR
IED TO CHEAT ME!":WEALTH=0:SUIT=0:LIGHT=
0:AXE=0:SWORD=0:AMULET=0:FOOD=INT(FOOD/4
):GOSUB 3520
```

```
3200 IF Z<>4 THEN 3030
3210 INPUT "HOW MANY UNITS OF FOOD";Q:Q=
INT(Q)
3220 IF 2*Q>WEALTH THEN PRINT "YOU HAVEN
'T GOT ENOUGH MONEY":GOTO 3210
3230 FOOD=FOOD+Q
3240 WEALTH=WEALTH-2*Q
3250 GOTO 3030
3260 IF WEALTH>0 THEN PRINT:PRINT:PRINT
"YOU HAVE $";WEALTH
3270 IF WEALTH=0 THEN PRINT "YOU HAVE NO
 MONEY":GOSUB 3520:RETURN
3280 FOR J=1 TO 4:PRINT:NEXT J
3290 RETURN
3300 REM ******************
3310 DATA 0,2,0,0,0,0,0:REM ROOM 1
3320 DATA 1,3,3,0,0,0,0:REM ROOM 2
3330 DATA 2,0,5,2,0,0,0:REM ROOM 3
3340 DATA 0,5,0,0,0,0,0:REM ROOM 4
3350 DATA 4,0,0,3,15,13,0:REM ROOM 5
3360 DATA 0,0,1,0,0,0,0: REM ROOM 6
3370 DATA 0,8,0,0,0,0,0: REM ROOM 7
3380 DATA 7,10,0,0,0,0,0: REM ROOM 8
3390 DATA 0,19,0,8,0,8,0:REM ROOM 9
3400 DATA 8,0,11,0,0,0,0:REM ROOM 10
3410 DATA 0,0,10,0,0,0,0:REM ROOM 11
3420 DATA 0,0,0,13,0,0,0:REM ROOM 12
3430 DATA 0,0,12,0,5,0,0:REM ROOM 13
3440 DATA 0,15,17,0,0,0,0:REM ROOM 14
3450 DATA 14,0,0,0,0,5,0:REM ROOM 15
3460 DATA 17,0,19,0,0,0,0:REM ROOM 16
3470 DATA 18,16,0,14,0,0,0:REM ROOM 17
3480 DATA 0,17,0,0,0,0,0:REM ROOM 18
3490 DATA 9,0,16,0,0,0,0:REM ROOM 19
3500 REM ******************
3510 REM ADJUST LOOP BELOW TO YOUR SYSTE
M
3520 FOR T=1 TO 900:NEXT T
3530 RETURN
```

14

DRESSING IT UP

Elaborations

Once you have a program up and running properly, behaving in accordance with an external map, the job is not yet done. You can stop for a while with the program you have, and it should be a source of a great deal of enjoyment. However, an urge to elaborate the original program is likely to arise after a while.

You now have a reasonable version of WEREWOLVES AND WANDERER up and running on your system. You know the basics of creating Adventure games, and are probably well on the way to completing your first major epic.

There is still a lot which can be added to WEREWOLVES AND WANDERER to make it more enjoyable for players, and once I'd spent a few weeks with the program in its original form, I decided to tackle the job of dressing it up.

A complete listing of the improved version appears in the next chapter, while this chapter contains part of a sample run of the new program, so you can get an idea of what has been added.

You can easily modify your original listing by changing some lines, and adding others in between those of the first version.

It is best to compare your listing with the next one, line by line (especially in the room descriptions) to make sure you have entered all the modifications. To simplify this, here are the major changes I have made:

- The torch can be knocked out of your hand during a fight—905.
- Your weapons can also be knocked out of your hands during a fight—906, 907.

- More monsters have been added—415, 416, and 2920.
- Jewels and the like can be found, rather than just unidentified "treasure"—355, 357.
- Note that not all doors are now described explicitly, leaving more to the player's skill in determining where the exits are. As well as this, the rooms are described in much greater detail, and some factors are added which only appear from time to time. You should check all the room descriptions.
- You can call for a tally at any time during the course of a game, by entering "T" when asked for a command—706.
- There is a pretty effect (which you're sure to be able to elaborate still further) when the amulet is triggered—625.
- The Inventory routine now includes feedback on the objects you have bought—delete 3120 and 3130 and add 3131, 3133, 3134, and 3135. Other lines will have to be renumbered as 3136 and 3137.
- Your starting wealth and strength are now determined randomly at the start of each game—2620, 2630.

Sample Run

Here's a sample run of the elaborated version:

```
YOU CAN BUY 1 - FLAMING TORCH ($15)
            2 - AXE ($10)
            3 - SWORD ($20)
            4 - FOOD ($2 PER UNIT)
            5 - MAGIC AMULET ($30)
            6 - SUIT OF ARMOR ($50)
            0 - TO CONTINUE ADVENTURE
YOU HAVE A TORCH

ENTER NO. OF ITEM REQUIRED? 2


YOU HAVE $ 9
```

YOU HAVE A TORCH
YOUR SUPPLIES NOW INCLUDE ONE AXE

ANDREW, YOUR STRENGTH IS 107
YOU HAVE $ 9
YOU ARE CARRYING AN AXE

****

YOU ARE IN THE HALLWAY
FROM THE DUST ON THE GROUND YOU CAN TELL
NO-ONE HAS WALKED HERE FOR A LONG, LONG TIME
THERE IS A DOOR TO THE SOUTH
THROUGH WINDOWS TO THE NORTH YOU CAN SEE A SECRET
HERB GARDEN
THERE IS TREASURE HERE WORTH $ 100

WHAT DO YOU WANT TO DO? P

****

YOU ARE IN THE GREAT HALL, AN L-SHAPED ROOM
THERE ARE TWO DOORS IN THIS ROOM
THE WOOD PANELS ARE WARPED AND FADED...
AS YOU STAND THERE, YOU HEAR A MOUSE SCAMPER ALONG
THE FLOOR BEHIND YOU...
YOU WHIRL AROUND...BUT SEE NOTHING!

DANGER...THERE IS A MONSTER HERE....

```
IT IS A DEVASTATING ICE-DRAGON

THE DANGER LEVEL IS 20 !!


WHAT DO YOU WANT TO DO? F

YOU MANAGE TO WOUND IT
*&%%$#$% $%# !!@ #$$#  #$@!  #$ $#$
WILL THIS BE A BATTLE TO THE DEATH?
HE STRIKES WILDLY, MADLY...........

THE MONSTER WOUNDS YOU!

THE DEVASTATING ICE-DRAGON DEFEATED YOU


ANDREW, YOUR STRENGTH IS 28
YOU HAVE $ 23
YOU ARE CARRYING THE MAGIC AMULET


******************************


YOU ARE IN THE GREAT HALL, AN L-SHAPED ROOM
THERE ARE TWO DOORS IN THIS ROOM
THE WOOD PANELS ARE WARPED AND FADED...


WHAT DO YOU WANT TO DO? M
```

*

*

*

```
                    *
                     *
                      *
                       *

ANDREW, YOUR STRENGTH IS 23
YOU HAVE $ 23
YOU ARE CARRYING THE MAGIC AMULET


******************************


YOU ARE IN THE REAR VESTIBULE
THERE ARE WINDOWS TO THE SOUTH FROM WHICH YOU
YOU CAN SEE THE ORNAMENTAL LAKE
```

From these "snapshots" you have probably gained a taste of how the original program has been greatly elaborated. I've tried to ensure—and this may be worth keeping in mind when you're working on your own programs—that any elaboration is not added purely for its own sake. Instead, you should decide whether or not to add further "frills" to a program purely in terms of whether or not they add to the player's experience of reality, excitement, and involvement when playing the game.

15

IMPROVED VERSION

Here's the complete listing of the revised version of WEREWOLVES AND WANDERER.

```
10 REM WEREWOLVES AND WANDERER
11 REM UPGRADED VERSION
20 GOSUB 2600:REM INITIALISE
30 GOSUB 160
40 IF RO <> 11 THEN 30
50 PRINT:PRINT "YOU'VE DONE IT!!":GOSUB 3
520:PRINT "THAT WAS THE EXIT FROM THE CAS
TLE"
60 GOSUB 3520
70 PRINT:PRINT "YOU HAVE SUCCEEDED, ";N$;
"!"
80 PRINT:PRINT "YOU MANAGED TO GET OUT OF
 THE CASTLE"
90 GOSUB 3520
100 PRINT:PRINT "WELL DONE!"
110 GOSUB 3520
120 PRINT:PRINT "YOUR SCORE IS";
130 PRINT 3*TALLY + 5*STRENGTH + 2*WEALTH
 + FOOD + 30*MK
140 END
150 REM ***********************
160 REM MAJOR HANDLING ROUTINE
170 STRENGTH = STRENGTH - 5
```

```
180 IF STRENGTH<10 THEN PRINT "WARNING, "
;N$;", YOUR STRENGTH":PRINT "IS RUNNING L
OW":PRINT
190 IF STRENGTH < 1 THEN 2300:REM DEATH
200 TALLY = TALLY + 1
210 PRINT N$;", YOUR STRENGTH IS";STRENGT
H
220 IF WEALTH > 0 THEN PRINT "YOU HAVE $"
;WEALTH
230 IF FOOD > 0 THEN PRINT "YOUR PROVISIO
NS SACK HOLDS";FOOD;"UNITS OF FOOD"
240 IF SUIT = 1 THEN PRINT "YOU ARE WEARI
NG ARMOR"
250 IF AXE=0 AND SWORD=0 AND AMULET=0 THE
N 320
260 PRINT "YOU ARE CARRYING ";
270 IF AXE=1 THEN PRINT "AN AXE ";
280 IF SWORD=1 THEN PRINT "A SWORD ";
290 IF SWORD + AXE > 0 AND AMULET=1 THEN
PRINT "AND ";
300 IF AMULET=1 THEN PRINT "THE MAGIC AMU
LET"
310 PRINT
320 IF LIGHT=0 THEN PRINT "IT IS TOO DARK
 TO SEE ANYTHING"
330 IF LIGHT=1 THEN GOSUB 990:REM ROOM DE
SCRIPTION
340 K = A(RO,7):REM K IS SET TO CONTENTS
OF ROOM
350 IF K=0 THEN 440:REM ROOM IS EMPTY
355 M=RND(1)
357 IF K>9 AND M<=.5 THEN PRINT "THERE AR
E GEMS HERE WORTH $";K:GOTO 440
360 IF K>9 AND M>.5 THEN PRINT "THERE IS
TREASURE HERE WORTH $";K:GOTO 440
370 PRINT:PRINT:PRINT "DANGER...THERE IS
A MONSTER HERE....":GOSUB 3520
380 IF K=-1 THEN M$="FEROCIOUS WEREWOLF":
FF=5
390 IF K=-2 THEN M$="FANATICAL FLESHGORGE
R":FF=10
400 IF K=-3 THEN M$="MALOVENTY MALDEMER":
FF=15
410 IF K=-4 THEN M$="DEVASTATING ICE-DRAG
```

```
ON":FF=20
415 IF K=-5 THEN M$="HORRENDOUS HODGEPODG
ER":FF=25
416 IF K=-6 THEN M$="GHASTLY GRUESOMENESS
":FF=30
420 PRINT:PRINT "IT IS A ";M$
430 PRINT:PRINT "THE DANGER LEVEL IS";FF;
"!!"
440 GOSUB 3520
450 PRINT:PRINT:PRINT "WHAT DO YOU WANT T
O DO";
460 INPUT A$:A$=LEFT$(A$,1)
470 IF K<0 AND A$<>"F" AND A$<>"R" THEN 4
60
480 PRINT:PRINT:PRINT "------------------
-------------------":PRINT
490 IF A$="Q" THEN 120
500 IF A$="N" AND A(RO,1)=0 THEN PRINT "N
O EXIT THAT WAY":GOTO 440
510 IF A$="S" AND A(RO,2)=0 THEN PRINT "T
HERE IS NO EXIT SOUTH":GOTO 440
520 IF A$="E" AND A(RO,3)=0 THEN PRINT "Y
OU CANNOT GO IN THAT DIRECTION":GOTO 440
530 IF A$="W" AND A(RO,4)=0 THEN PRINT "Y
OU CANNOT MOVE THROUGH SOLID STONE":GOTO
440
540 IF A$="U" AND A(RO,5)=0 THEN PRINT "T
HERE IS NO WAY UP FROM HERE":GOTO 440
550 IF A$="D" AND A(RO,6)=0 THEN PRINT "Y
OU CANNOT DESCEND FROM HERE":GOTO 440
560 IF A$="R" AND RND(1)>.7 THEN 2420
570 IF A$="R" THEN K=0:PRINT "WHICH WAY DO
 YOU WANT TO FLEE";:GOTO 460
580 IF A$="F" AND A(RO,7)>-1 THEN PRINT "
THERE IS NOTHING TO FIGHT HERE":GOTO 440
590 IF A$="I" THEN GOSUB 3010:RETURN
600 IF A$="C" AND FOOD=0 THEN PRINT "YOU
HAVE NO FOOD":GOTO 440
610 IF A$="P" THEN GOSUB 2350:RETURN
620 IF A$="F" THEN 730
625 IF A$="M" THEN FOR J = 1 TO 30:PRINT
TAB(J);"*":NEXT J
630 IF A$="M" THEN RO=INT(RND(1)*19)+1:IF
 RO=6 OR RO=11 THEN 630 ELSE 710
```

```
640 IF A$="C" THEN GOSUB 2480:RETURN
650 IF A$="N" THEN RO=A(RO,1)
660 IF A$="S" THEN RO=A(RO,2)
670 IF A$="E" THEN RO=A(RO,3)
680 IF A$="W" THEN RO=A(RO,4)
690 IF A$="U" THEN RO=A(RO,5)
700 IF A$="D" THEN RO=A(RO,6)
705 IF A$="T" THEN PRINT "YOUR TALLY AT P
RESENT IS";3*TALLY + 5*STRENGTH + 2*WEALT
H + FOOD + 30*MK
706 IF A$="T" AND RND>.5 THEN PRINT:PRINT
 "YOU HAVE KILLED";MK;"MONSTERS SO FAR...
"
710 RETURN
720 REM **************************
730 REM FIGHT
740 IF INKEY$<>"" THEN 740
750 PRINT "PRESS ANY KEY TO FIGHT"
760 IF INKEY$="" THEN 760
770 IF SUIT=1 THEN PRINT "YOUR ARMOR INCR
EASES YOUR CHANCE OF SUCCESS":FF=3*(INT(F
F/4)):GOSUB 3520
780 CLS:FOR J=1 TO 6:PRINT "*_*_*_*_*_*_*
_*_*_*_*_*_*_*_*_*_*_*_*_*":NEXT J
790 IF AXE=0 AND SWORD=0 THEN PRINT "YOU
HAVE NO WEAPONS":PRINT "YOU MUST FIGHT WI
TH BARE HANDS":FF=INT(FF + FF/5):GOTO 870

800 IF AXE=1 AND SWORD=0 THEN PRINT "YOU
HAVE ONLY AN AXE TO FIGHT WITH":FF=4*INT(
FF/5):GOTO 870
810 IF AXE=0 AND SWORD=1 THEN PRINT "YOU
MUST FIGHT WITH YOUR SWORD":FF=3*INT(FF/4
):GOTO 870
820 INPUT "WHICH WEAPON? 1 - AXE, 2 - SWO
RD";Z
830 IF Z<1 OR Z>2 THEN 820
840 IF Z=1 THEN FF=4*INT(FF/5)
850 IF Z=2 THEN FF=3*INT(FF/4)
860 REM *************************
870 REM THE BATTLE
880 PRINT:PRINT
890 IF RND(1)>.5 THEN PRINT M$;" ATTACKS"
 ELSE PRINT "YOU ATTACK"
```

```
900 GOSUB 3520
905 IF RND>.5 AND LIGHT=1 THEN PRINT "YOU
R TORCH WAS KNOCKED FROM YOUR HAND":LIGHT
=0:GOSUB 3520
906 IF RND>.5 AND AXE=1 THEN PRINT "YOU D
ROP YOUR AXE IN THE HEAT OF BATTLE":AXE=0
:FF=5*INT(FF/4)
907 IF RND>.5 AND SWORD=1 THEN PRINT "YOU
R SWORD IS KNOCKED FROM YOUR HAND!!!":SWO
RD=0:FF=4*INT(FF/3)
910 IF RND(1)>.5 THEN PRINT:PRINT "YOU MA
NAGE TO WOUND IT":FF=INT(5*FF/6)
911 IF RND>.95 THEN PRINT "Aaaaargh!!!":G
OSUB 3520:PRINT "RIP! TEAR! RIP!"
912 IF RND>.9 THEN PRINT "YOU WANT TO RUN
, BUT YOU STAND YOUR GROUND..."
913 IF RND>.9 THEN PRINT "*&%%$#$% $%# !!
@ #$$#  #$@!  #$ $#$"
914 IF RND>.7 THEN PRINT "WILL THIS BE A
BATTLE TO THE DEATH?"
915 IF RND>.7 THEN PRINT "HIS EYES FLASH
FEARFULLY"
916 IF RND>.7 THEN PRINT "BLOOD DRIPS FRO
M HIS CLAWS"
917 IF RND>.7 THEN PRINT "YOU SMELL THE S
ULPHUR ON HIS BREATH"
918 IF RND>.7 THEN PRINT "HE STRIKES WILD
LY, MADLY.........."
919 IF RND>.7 THEN PRINT "YOU HAVE NEVER
FOUGHT AN OPPONENT LIKE THIS!!"
920 GOSUB 3520
930 IF RND(1)>.5 THEN PRINT:PRINT "THE MO
NSTER WOUNDS YOU!":STRENGTH=STRENGTH-5
940 IF RND(1)>.35 THEN 890
950 IF RND(1)*16>FF THEN PRINT:PRINT "AND
 YOU MANAGED TO KILL THE ";M$:MK=MK+1:GOT
O 970
960 PRINT:PRINT "THE ";M$;" DEFEATED YOU"
:STRENGTH=INT(STRENGTH/2)
970 A(RO,7)=0:GOSUB 3520:PRINT:PRINT:GOSU
B 3520:RETURN
980 REM *****************
990 REM ROOM DESCRIPTIONS
1000 PRINT:PRINT "************************
```

```
********":PRINT:PRINT
1010 ON RO GOSUB 1040,1100,1170,1230,1280
,1360,1410,1470,1540,1620,1700,1730,1790,
1860,1960,2030,2100,2160,2230
1020 RETURN
1030 REM *************
1040 REM ROOM 1
1050 PRINT "YOU ARE IN THE HALLWAY"
1055 IF RND>.4 THEN PRINT "FROM THE DUST
ON THE GROUND YOU CAN TELL":PRINT "NO-ONE
 HAS WALKED HERE FOR A LONG, LONG TIME"
1060 PRINT "THERE IS A DOOR TO THE SOUTH"

1070 PRINT "THROUGH WINDOWS TO THE NORTH
YOU CAN SEE A SECRET HERB GARDEN"
1080 RETURN
1090 REM *************
1100 REM ROOM 2
1110 PRINT "THIS IS THE AUDIENCE CHAMBER"

1115 IF RND>.4 THEN PRINT "THE FADED TAPE
STRIES ON THE WALL ONLY":PRINT "HINT AT T
HE SPLENDOR WHICH THIS ROOM ONCE HAD"
1120 PRINT "THERE IS A WINDOW TO THE WEST
. BY LOOKING TO THE RIGHT"
1130 PRINT "THROUGH IT YOU CAN SEE THE EN
TRANCE TO THE CASTLE."
1150 RETURN
1160 REM *************
1170 REM ROOM 3
1180 PRINT "YOU ARE IN THE GREAT HALL, AN
 L-SHAPED ROOM"
1190 PRINT "THERE ARE TWO DOORS IN THIS R
OOM"
1200 PRINT "THE WOOD PANELS ARE WARPED AN
D FADED..."
1205 IF RND>.4 THEN PRINT "AS YOU STAND T
HERE, YOU HEAR A MOUSE SCAMPER ALONG":PRI
NT "THE FLOOR BEHIND YOU...":PRINT "YOU W
HIRL AROUND...BUT SEE NOTHING!"
1210 RETURN
1220 REM *************
1230 REM ROOM 4
1240 PRINT "THIS IS THE MONARCH'S PRIVATE
```

```
 MEETING ROOM"
1245 IF RND < .4  THEN PRINT "THE ECHO OF
 ANCIENT PLOTTING AND WRANGLING HANGS":PR
INT "HEAVY IN THE MUSTY AIR..."
1250 PRINT "THERE IS A SINGLE EXIT TO THE
 SOUTH"
1260 RETURN
1270 REM *************
1280 REM ROOM 5
1290 PRINT "THIS INNER HALLWAY CONTAINS A
 DOOR TO THE NORTH,"
1300 PRINT "AND ONE TO THE WEST, AND A CI
RCULAR STAIRWELL"
1310 PRINT "PASSES THROUGH THE ROOM"
1315 IF RND >.6 THEN PRINT "THE ROOM IS S
MALL, AND UNFRIENDLY"
1320 PRINT "YOU CAN SEE AN ORNAMENTAL LAK
E THROUGH THE"
1330 PRINT "WINDOWS TO THE SOUTH"
1340 RETURN
1350 REM *************
1360 REM ROOM 6
1370 PRINT "YOU ARE AT THE ENTRANCE TO A
FORBIDDING-LOOKING"
1380 PRINT "STONE CASTLE.  YOU ARE FACING
 EAST"
1390 RETURN
1400 REM *************
1410 REM ROOM 7
1420 PRINT "THIS IS THE CASTLE'S KITCHEN.
 THROUGH WINDOWS IN"
1430 PRINT "THE NORTH WALL YOU CAN SEE A
SECRET HERB GARDEN."
1440 PRINT "IT HAS BEEN MANY YEARS SINCE
MEALS WERE"
1441 PRINT "PREPARED FOR THE MONARCH AND
THE COURT"
1442 PRINT "IN THIS KITCHEN......."
1443 IF RND>.4 THEN PRINT "...A RAT SCURR
IES ACROSS THE FLOOR..."
1450 RETURN
1460 REM ***************
1470 REM ROOM 8
1480 PRINT "YOU ARE IN THE STORE ROOM, AM
```

```
IDST SPICES,"
1490 PRINT "VEGETABLES, AND VAST SACKS OF
 FLOUR AND"
1500 PRINT "OTHER PROVISIONS."
1515 PRINT "THE AIR IS THICK WITH SPICE A
ND CURRY FUMES..."
1520 RETURN
1530 REM ***************
1540 REM ROOM 9
1550 PRINT "YOU HAVE ENTERED THE LIFT..."

1560 GOSUB 3520
1570 PRINT "IT SLOWLY DESCENDS..."
1580 GOSUB 3520
1590 RO=10
1600 GOTO 1000
1610 REM *************************
1620 REM ROOM 10
1630 PRINT "YOU ARE IN THE REAR VESTIBULE
"
1640 PRINT "THERE ARE WINDOWS TO THE SOUT
H FROM WHICH YOU"
1650 PRINT "YOU CAN SEE THE ORNAMENTAL LA
KE"
1660 PRINT "THERE IS AN EXIT TO THE EAST,
 AND"
1670 PRINT "ONE TO THE NORTH"
1680 RETURN
1690 REM *****************
1700 REM ROOM 11
1710 RETURN
1720 REM *****************
1730 REM ROOM 12
1740 PRINT "YOU ARE IN THE DANK, DARK DUN
GEON"
1750 PRINT "THERE IS A SINGLE EXIT, A SMA
LL HOLE IN"
1760 PRINT "WALL TOWARDS THE WEST"
1765 IF RND>.4 THEN PRINT "...A HOLLOW, D
RY CHUCKLE IS HEARD":PRINT "FROM THE GUAR
D ROOM...."
1770 RETURN
1780 REM *****************
1790 REM ROOM 13
```

```
1800 PRINT "YOU ARE IN THE PRISON GUARDRO
OM, IN THE"
1810 PRINT "BASEMENT OF THE CASTLE. THE S
TAIRWELL"
1820 PRINT "ENDS IN THIS ROOM. THERE IS O
NE OTHER"
1830 PRINT "EXIT, A SMALL HOLE IN THE EAS
T WALL"
1835 PRINT "THE AIR IS DAMP AND UNPLEASAN
T...A CHILL WIND"
1836 PRINT "RUSHES INTO THE ROOM FROM GAP
S IN THE STONE"
1837 PRINT "AT THE TOP OF THE WALLS"
1840 RETURN
1850 REM ****************
1860 REM ROOM 14
1870 PRINT "YOU ARE IN THE MASTER BEDROOM
 ON THE UPPER"
1880 PRINT "LEVEL OF THE CASTLE...."
1890 PRINT "LOOKING DOWN FROM THE WINDOW
TO THE WEST YOU"
1900 PRINT "CAN SEE THE ENTRANCE TO THE C
ASTLE, WHILE THE"
1910 PRINT "SECRET HERB GARDEN IS VISIBLE
 BELOW THE NORTH"
1920 PRINT "WINDOW. THERE ARE DOORS TO TH
E EAST AND"
1930 PRINT "TO THE SOUTH...."
1940 RETURN
1950 REM ****************
1960 REM ROOM 15
1970 PRINT "THIS IS THE L-SHAPED UPPER HA
LLWAY."
1971 IF RND>.4 THEN PRINT "...A MOTH FLIT
S ACROSS NEAR THE CEILING..."
1980 PRINT "TO THE NORTH IS A DOOR, AND T
HERE IS A"
1990 PRINT "STAIRWELL IN THE HALL AS WELL
. YOU CAN SEE"
2000 PRINT "THE LAKE THROUGH THE SOUTH WI
NDOWS"
2010 RETURN
2020 REM ****************
2030 REM ROOM 16
```

```
2040 PRINT "THIS ROOM WAS USED AS THE CAS
TLE TREASURY IN"
2050 PRINT "BY-GONE YEARS...."
2055 IF RND>.4 THEN PRINT "...A SPIDER SC
AMPERS DOWN THE WALL......."
2060 PRINT "THERE ARE NO WINDOWS, JUST EX
ITS."
2080 RETURN
2090 REM **************
2100 REM ROOM 17
2110 PRINT "OOOOH...YOU ARE IN THE CHAMBE
RMAIDS' BEDROOM"
2115 PRINT "FAINT PERFUME STILL HANGS IN
THE AIR..."
2120 PRINT "THERE IS AN EXIT TO THE WEST
AND A DOOR"
2130 PRINT "TO THE SOUTH...."
2140 RETURN
2150 REM ***************
2160 REM ROOM 18
2170 PRINT "THIS TINY ROOM ON THE UPPER L
EVEL IS THE"
2180 PRINT "DRESSING CHAMBER. THERE IS A
WINDOW TO THE"
2190 PRINT "NORTH, WITH A VIEW OF THE HER
B GARDEN DOWN"
2200 PRINT "BELOW. A DOOR LEAVES TO THE S
OUTH"
2210 RETURN
2215 PRINT "YOU CATCH A GLIMPSE OF YOURSE
LF IN THE MIRROR"
2216 PRINT "HANGING ON THE WALL AND ARE S
HOCKED AT YOUR"
2217 PRINT "DISHEVELED APPEARANCE"
2220 REM *************
2230 REM ROOM 19
2240 PRINT "THIS IS THE SMALL ROOM OUTSID
E THE CASTLE"
2260 PRINT "YOU CAN SEE.................
...."
2270 PRINT "THE LAKE THROUGH THE SOUTHERN
 WINDOWS"
2280 RETURN
2290 REM **************
```

```
2300 REM DEAD END
2310 PRINT "YOU HAVE DIED........."
2320 GOSUB 3520
2330 GOTO 120
2340 REM ***************
2350 REM PICK UP TREASURE
2360 IF A(RO,7)<10 THEN PRINT "THERE IS N
O TREASURE TO PICK UP":GOSUB 3520:RETURN
2370 IF LIGHT=0 THEN PRINT "YOU CANNOT SE
E WHERE IT IS":GOSUB 3520:RETURN
2380 WEALTH=WEALTH + A(RO,7)
2390 A(RO,7)=0
2400 RETURN
2410 REM ***************
2420 REM UNSUCCESSFUL ATTEMPT TO RUN
2430 PRINT "NO YOU MUST STAND AND FIGHT"
2440 A$="F"
2450 GOSUB 3520
2460 GOTO 590
2470 REM ***************
2480 REM EAT FOOD
2490 CLS
2500 IF FOOD<1 THEN RETURN
2510 PRINT "YOU HAVE";FOOD;"UNITS OF FOOD
"
2520 PRINT "HOW MANY DO YOU WANT TO EAT";

2530 INPUT Z
2540 IF Z>FOOD THEN 2530
2550 FOOD=INT(FOOD-Z)
2560 STRENGTH=INT(STRENGTH+5*Z)
2570 GOSUB 3410:CLS
2580 RETURN
2590 REM ***********
2600 REM INITIALISE
2610 CLS
2620 STRENGTH= 60 + INT(RND(1)*100)
2630 WEALTH= 30 + INT(RND(1)*100)
2640 FOOD=0
2650 TALLY=0
2660 MK=0:REM NO. OF MONSTERS KILLED
2670 REM ***************
2680 REM SET UP CASTLE
2690 DIM A(19,7)
```

```
2700 FOR B=1 TO 19
2710 FOR C=1 TO 7
2720 READ A(B,C)
2730 NEXT C
2740 NEXT B
2750 INPUT "WHAT IS YOUR NAME, EXPLORER";
N$
2760 CLS
2770 RO=6:REM STARTING POSITION (RO=ROOM
NUMBER)
2780 SWORD=0
2790 AMULET=0
2800 AXE=0
2810 SUIT=0
2820 LIGHT=0
2830 REM ***************
2840 REM ALLOT TREASURE
2850 FOR J = 1 TO 4
2860 M=INT(RND(1)*19)+1
2870 IF M=6 OR M=11 OR A(M,7)<>0 THEN 286
0
2880 A(M,7)=INT(RND(1)*100)+10
2890 NEXT J
2900 REM ***************
2910 REM ALLOT MONSTERS
2920 FOR J=1 TO 6
2930 M=INT(RND(1)*18)+1
2940 IF M=6 OR M=11 OR A(M,7)<>0 THEN 293
0
2950 A(M,7)= -J
2960 NEXT J
2970 A(4,7)=100+INT(RND(1)*100)
2980 A(16,7)=100+INT(RND(1)*100)
2990 RETURN
3000 REM ******************************
3010 REM INVENTORY/PROVISIONS
3020 PRINT "PROVISIONS & INVENTORY"
3030 GOSUB 3260
3040 IF WEALTH<.1 THEN Z=0:GOTO 3137
3050 PRINT "YOU CAN BUY 1 - FLAMING TORCH
 ($15)"
3060 PRINT "                2 - AXE ($10)"
3070 PRINT "                3 - SWORD ($20)"
3080 PRINT "                4 - FOOD ($2 PER
```

```
UNIT)"
3090 PRINT "                    5 - MAGIC AMULET
($30)"
3100 PRINT "                    6 - SUIT OF ARMOR
 ($50)"
3110 PRINT "                    0 - TO CONTINUE A
DVENTURE"
3131 IF LIGHT=1 THEN PRINT "YOU HAVE A TO
RCH"
3132 IF AXE=1 THEN PRINT "YOUR SUPPLIES N
OW INCLUDE ONE AXE"
3133 IF SWORD=1 THEN PRINT "YOU SHOULD GU
ARD YOUR SWORD WELL"
3134 IF AMULET=1 THEN PRINT "YOUR AMULET
WILL AID YOU IN TIMES OF STRESS"
3135 IF SUIT=1 THEN PRINT "YOU LOOK GOOD
IN ARMOR"
3136 PRINT:INPUT "ENTER NO. OF ITEM REQUI
RED";Z
3137 IF Z=0 THEN CLS:RETURN
3140 IF Z=1 THEN LIGHT=1:WEALTH=WEALTH-15

3150 IF Z=2 THEN AXE=1:WEALTH=WEALTH-10
3160 IF Z=3 THEN SWORD=1:WEALTH=WEALTH-20

3170 IF Z=5 THEN AMULET=1:WEALTH=WEALTH-3
0
3180 IF Z=6 THEN SUIT=1:WEALTH=WEALTH-50
3190 IF WEALTH<0 THEN PRINT "YOU HAVE TRI
ED TO CHEAT ME!":WEALTH=0:SUIT=0:LIGHT=0:
AXE=0:SWORD=0:AMULET=0:FOOD=INT(FOOD/4):G
OSUB 3520
3200 IF Z<>4 THEN 3030
3210 INPUT "HOW MANY UNITS OF FOOD";Q:Q=I
NT(Q)
3220 IF 2*Q>WEALTH THEN PRINT "YOU HAVEN'
T GOT ENOUGH MONEY":GOTO 3210
3230 FOOD=FOOD+Q
3240 WEALTH=WEALTH-2*Q
3250 GOTO 3030
3260 IF WEALTH>0 THEN PRINT:PRINT:PRINT "
YOU HAVE $";WEALTH
3270 IF WEALTH=0 THEN PRINT "YOU HAVE NO
MONEY":GOSUB 3520:RETURN
```

```
3280 FOR J=1 TO 4:PRINT:NEXT J
3290 RETURN
3300 REM *******************
3310 DATA 0,2,0,0,0,0,0:REM ROOM 1
3320 DATA 1,3,3,0,0,0,0:REM ROOM 2
3330 DATA 2,0,5,2,0,0,0:REM ROOM 3
3340 DATA 0,5,0,0,0,0,0:REM ROOM 4
3350 DATA 4,0,0,3,15,13,0:REM ROOM 5
3360 DATA 0,0,1,0,0,0,0: REM ROOM 6
3370 DATA 0,8,0,0,0,0,0: REM ROOM 7
3380 DATA 7,10,0,0,0,0,0: REM ROOM 8
3390 DATA 0,19,0,8,0,8,0:REM ROOM 9
3400 DATA 8,0,11,0,0,0,0:REM ROOM 10
3410 DATA 0,0,10,0,0,0,0:REM ROOM 11
3420 DATA 0,0,0,13,0,0,0:REM ROOM 12
3430 DATA 0,0,12,0,5,0,0:REM ROOM 13
3440 DATA 0,15,17,0,0,0,0:REM ROOM 14
3450 DATA 14,0,0,0,0,5,0:REM ROOM 15
3460 DATA 17,0,19,0,0,0,0:REM ROOM 16
3470 DATA 18,16,0,14,0,0,0:REM ROOM 17
3480 DATA 0,17,0,0,0,0,0:REM ROOM 18
3490 DATA 9,0,16,0,0,0,0:REM ROOM 19
3500 REM *******************
3510 REM ADJUST LOOP BELOW TO YOUR SYSTEM

3520 FOR T=1 TO 900:NEXT T
3530 RETURN
```

16

TAKING IT TO THE SPACE LANES

You now have one or two working Adventure programs. What you also have, although you may not have realized it, is a shell or framework within which you can create your own Adventure.

Rather than having to go to the trouble of starting completely from scratch, you can simply modify the program to create a totally original Adventure program of your own. The DATA statements which define the map, and the PRINT statements which describe the rooms, are the main areas which must be changed.

However, as I'm sure you are pleased to learn, the rest of the program, which makes up the mechanism which keeps the Adventure moving, can be left more or less the same.

The New Scenario

To demonstrate just how very effective this "creation/modificaton" can be, I decided to take the first (not the elaborated version) WEREWOLVES AND WANDERER, and turn it into an Adventure out in space. The scenario is as follows. The intergalactic liner, *The Isaac Asimov,* met with an unexplained disaster when on its way, with over 1,000 passengers, to the terraformed planets of the Seuxarian System.

When out on your regular patrol of the space lanes, two centuries later, you come across the drifting hulk of *The Isaac Asimov.* You decide to explore, to see if you can determine what went wrong. However, no sooner have you entered the hold of the wrecked ship than your own ship, which you left tethered outside, explodes. You must find a Safety-Pod on board the *Asimov*, or die.

In this Adventure, you explore the wrecked ship, fight off androids and aliens, and face a few other problems which I will explain to you after you've played the game.

I will not let you see the map at this stage (and I hope you won't peek at it further on in the book), because by now you should be quite adept at deducing the map upon which the game is based.

There are several tricks and traps in this new Adventure, which make it relatively hard to solve, but you are sure to enjoy having a bigger problem to sink your teeth into.

Sample Run

Here's part of a sample run of The Aftermath of the Asimovian Disaster:

```
WHAT IS YOUR NAME, SPACE HERO? ANDREW

CAPTAIN ANDREW, YOUR STRENGTH IS 101
YOU HAVE $ 59 IN SOLARIAN CREDITS
YOUR RESERVE TANKS HOLD 10 UNITS OF OXYGEN
IT IS TOO DARK TO SEE ANYTHING
THERE IS TREASURE HERE WORTH $ 75



WHAT DO YOU WANT TO DO? I

 A SUPPLY ANDROID HAS ARRIVED

YOU HAVE $ 59 IN SOLARIAN CREDITS

YOU CAN BUY 1 - NUCLEONIC LIGHT ($15)
            2 - ION GUN ($10)
            3 - LASER ($20)
            4 - OXYGEN ($2 PER UNIT)
            5 - MATTER TRANSPORTER ($30)
            6 - COMBAT SUIT ($50)
            0 - TO CONTINUE EXPLORATION
```

```
ENTER NO. OF ITEM REQUIRED? 1


CAPTAIN ANDREW, YOUR STRENGTH IS 96
YOU HAVE $ 24 IN SOLARIAN CREDITS
YOUR RESERVE TANKS HOLD 10 UNITS OF OXYGEN
YOU ARE CARRYING A LASER

********************************



YOU ARE IN THE WRECKED HOLD OF A SPACESHIP
THE CAVERNOUS INTERIOR IS LITTERED WITH
FLOATING WRECKAGE, AS IF FROM SOME
TERRIBLE EXPLOSION EONS AGO......
THERE IS TREASURE HERE WORTH $ 75


********************************



YOU ARE IN THE CREW'S SLEEPING QUARTERS
MOST OF THE SLEEPING SHELLS ARE EMPTY
THE FEW REMAINING CREW STIR FITFULLY
IN THEIR ENDLESS, DREAMLESS SLEEP



DANGER...THERE IS DANGER HERE....

IT IS A SNIGGERING GREEN ALIEN

YOUR PERSONAL DANGER METER REGISTERS 20 !!


WHAT DO YOU WANT TO DO? F
```

```
YOU MUST FIGHT WITH YOUR LASER


SNIGGERING GREEN ALIEN ATTACKS

THE SNIGGERING GREEN ALIEN WOUNDS YOU!
YOU ATTACK

THE SNIGGERING GREEN ALIEN WOUNDS YOU!
SNIGGERING GREEN ALIEN ATTACKS

THE SNIGGERING GREEN ALIEN WOUNDS YOU!
YOU ATTACK

THE SNIGGERING GREEN ALIEN SERIOUSLY WOUNDS YOU

THIS IS THE SHIP'S HOSPITAL, WHITE AND STERILE.
A BUZZING SOUND, AND A STRANGE WARMTH COME FROM
THE SOUTH, WHILE A CHILL IS FELT TO THE NORTH
```

I'm sure you can see quite clearly how this program is related to WEREWOLVES AND WANDERER. However, despite its obvious derivation from the first program, you'll see that it provides a completely different set of challenges to the player, and evokes a whole new area of mental images.

The complete listing of the AFTERMATH OF THE ASIMOVIAN DISASTER is presented in the next chapter.

17

THE ASIMOVIAN LISTING

Remember, this program is based on the first, unelaborated version of WEREWOLVES AND WANDERER. You can simply load up the very first program, and then work through it—section by section—to create the new program.

Note that in all cases FOOD is changed to OXY, AXE becomes ION, SWORD is changed to LASER, and AMULET becomes TRANSPORTER. The command "B" (related to your oxygen use) has been added to your vocabulary.

```
10 REM AFTERMATH OF THE ASIMOVIAN DISAST
ER
20 GOSUB 2600:REM INITIALISE
30 GOSUB 160
35 IF RO=13 THEN QQ=QQ+1:IF QQ=2 THEN 13
85
40 GOTO 30
150 REM ************************
160 REM MAJOR HANDLING ROUTINE
170 STRENGTH = STRENGTH - 5
180 IF STRENGTH<10 THEN PRINT "WARNING,
CAPTAIN ";N$;", YOUR STRENGTH":PRINT "IS
 RUNNING LOW":PRINT"YOU NEED AN OXYGEN B
OOST"
190 IF STRENGTH < 1 THEN 2300:REM DEATH
200 TALLY = TALLY + 1
210 PRINT "CAPTAIN ";N$;", YOUR STRENGTH
 IS";STRENGTH
```

```
220 IF WEALTH > 0 THEN PRINT "YOU HAVE $
";WEALTH;"IN SOLARIAN CREDITS"
230 IF OXY>0 THEN PRINT "YOUR RESERVE TA
NKS HOLD";OXY;"UNITS OF OXYGEN"
240 IF SUIT = 1 THEN PRINT "YOU ARE WEAR
ING BATTLE ARMOR"
250 IF ION=0 AND LASER=0 AND TRANSPORTER
=0 THEN 320
260 PRINT "YOU ARE CARRYING ";
270 IF ION=1 THEN PRINT "AN ION GUN ";
280 IF LASER=1 THEN PRINT "A LASER ";
290 IF LASER + ION > 0 AND TRANSPORTER=1
 THEN PRINT "AND ";
300 IF TRANSPORTER=1 THEN PRINT "THE MAT
TER TRANSPORTER"
310 PRINT
320 IF LIGHT=0 THEN PRINT "IT IS TOO DAR
K TO SEE ANYTHING"
330 IF LIGHT=1 THEN GOSUB 990:REM ROOM D
ESCRIPTION
340 K = A(RO,7):REM K IS SET TO CONTENTS
 OF ROOM
350 IF K=0 THEN 440:REM ROOM IS EMPTY
360 IF K>9 THEN PRINT "THERE IS TREASURE
 HERE WORTH $";K:GOTO 440
370 PRINT:PRINT:PRINT "DANGER...THERE IS
 DANGER HERE....":GOSUB 3520
380 IF K=-1 THEN M$="BERSERK ANDROID":FF
=5
390 IF K=-2 THEN M$="DERANGED DEL-FIEVIA
N":FF=10
400 IF K=-3 THEN M$="RAMPAGING ROBOTIC D
EVICE":FF=15
410 IF K=-4 THEN M$="SNIGGERING GREEN AL
IEN":FF=20
420 PRINT:PRINT "IT IS A ";M$
430 PRINT:PRINT "YOUR PERSONAL DANGER ME
TER REGISTERS";FF;"!!"
440 GOSUB 3520
450 PRINT:PRINT:PRINT "WHAT DO YOU WANT
TO DO";
460 INPUT A$:A$=LEFT$(A$,1)
470 IF K<0 AND A$<>"F" AND A$<>"R" THEN
460
```

```
480 PRINT:PRINT:PRINT "-----------------
-------------------":PRINT
490 IF A$="Q" THEN 120
500 IF A$="N" AND A(RO,1)=0 THEN PRINT "
NO EXIT THAT WAY":GOTO 440
510 IF A$="S" AND A(RO,2)=0 THEN PRINT "
THERE IS NO EXIT SOUTH":GOTO 440
520 IF A$="E" AND A(RO,3)=0 THEN PRINT "
YOU CANNOT GO IN THAT DIRECTION":GOTO 44
0
530 IF A$="W" AND A(RO,4)=0 THEN PRINT "
YOU CANNOT MOVE THROUGH SOLID WALLS":GOT
O 440
540 IF A$="U" AND A(RO,5)=0 THEN PRINT "
THERE IS NO WAY UP FROM HERE":GOTO 440
550 IF A$="D" AND A(RO,6)=0 THEN PRINT "
YOU CANNOT DESCEND FROM HERE":GOTO 440
560 IF A$="R" AND RND(1)>.7 THEN 2420
570 IF A$="R" THEN K=0:PRINT "WHICH WAY
DO YOU WANT TO RUN";:GOTO 460
580 IF A$="F" AND A(RO,7)>-1 THEN PRINT
"THERE IS NOTHING TO FIGHT HERE":GOTO 44
0
590 IF A$="I" THEN GOSUB 3010:RETURN
600 IF A$="B" AND OXY=0 THEN PRINT "YOU
HAVE NO OXYGEN":GOTO 440
610 IF A$="P" THEN GOSUB 2350:RETURN
620 IF A$="F" THEN 730
625 IF A$="M" AND RO=13 THEN PRINT "THAT
 IS NOT POSSIBLE":GOSUB 3520:GOTO 450
630 IF A$="M" THEN RO=INT(RND(1)*19)+1:I
F RO=6 OR RO=11 THEN 630 ELSE 710
640 IF A$="B" THEN GOSUB 2480:RETURN
650 IF A$="N" THEN RO=A(RO,1)
660 IF A$="S" THEN RO=A(RO,2)
670 IF A$="E" THEN RO=A(RO,3)
680 IF A$="W" THEN RO=A(RO,4)
690 IF A$="U" THEN RO=A(RO,5)
700 IF A$="D" THEN RO=A(RO,6)
710 RETURN
720 REM ****************************
730 REM FIGHT
740 IF INKEY$<>"" THEN 740
750 PRINT "PRESS ANY KEY TO FIGHT"
```

```
760 IF INKEY$="" THEN 760
770 IF SUIT=1 THEN PRINT "YOUR SPACE-ARM
OR INCREASES YOUR CHANCE OF SUCCESS":FF=
3*(INT(FF/4)):GOSUB 3520
780 CLS:FOR J=1 TO INT(RND(1)*6)+1:PRINT
 "*_*_*_*_*_*_*_*_*_*_*_*_*_*_*_*_*_*_*_
*":NEXT J
785 PRINT
790 IF ION=0 AND LASER=0 THEN PRINT "YOU
 HAVE NO WEAPONS":PRINT "YOU MUST FIGHT
WITH BARE HANDS":FF=INT(FF + FF/5):GOTO
870
800 IF ION=1 AND LASER=0 THEN PRINT "YOU
 HAVE ONLY THE ION GUN TO FIGHT WITH":FF
=4*INT(FF/5):GOTO 870
810 IF ION=0 AND LASER=1 THEN PRINT "YOU
 MUST FIGHT WITH YOUR LASER":FF=3*INT(FF
/4):GOTO 870
820 INPUT "WHICH WEAPON? 1 - ION GUN, 2
- LASER";Z
830 IF Z<1 OR Z>2 THEN 820
840 IF Z=1 THEN FF=4*INT(FF/5)
850 IF Z=2 THEN FF=3*INT(FF/4)
860 REM ***************************
870 REM THE BATTLE
880 PRINT:PRINT
890 IF RND(1)>.5 THEN PRINT M$;" ATTACKS
" ELSE PRINT "YOU ATTACK"
900 GOSUB 3520
910 IF RND(1)>.5 THEN PRINT:PRINT "YOU G
ET THE ";M$;" A GLANCING BLOW":FF=INT(5*
FF/6)
920 GOSUB 3520
930 IF RND(1)>.5 THEN PRINT:PRINT "THE "
;M$;" WOUNDS YOU!":STRENGTH=STRENGTH-5
940 IF RND(1)>.35 THEN 890
950 IF RND(1)*16>FF THEN PRINT:PRINT "AN
D YOU MANAGE TO KILL THE ";M$:MK=MK+1:GO
TO 970
960 PRINT:PRINT "THE ";M$;" SERIOUSLY WO
UNDS YOU":STRENGTH=INT(STRENGTH/2)
970 A(RO,7)=0:GOSUB 3410:PRINT:PRINT:GOS
UB 3520:RETURN
980 REM *****************
```

```
990 REM ROOM DESCRIPTIONS
1000 PRINT:PRINT "************************
********":PRINT:PRINT
1010 ON RO GOSUB 1040,1100,1170,1230,128
0,1360,1410,1470,1540,1620,1700,1730,179
0,1860,1960,2030,2100,2160,2230
1020 RETURN
1030 REM ************
1040 REM ROOM 1
1050 PRINT "YOU ARE IN THE FORMER RECREA
TION"
1060 PRINT "CENTER. EQUIPMENT FOR MUSCLE
-TRAINING"
1070 PRINT "IN ZERO GRAVITY LITTERS THE
AREA"
1080 RETURN
1090 REM ************
1100 REM ROOM 2
1110 PRINT "THIS WAS THE REPAIR AND MAIN
TENANCE"
1120 PRINT "HOLD OF THE SHIP. YOU CAN ON
LY LEAVE IT"
1130 PRINT "VIA THE GIANT HANGAR DOOR TO
 THE WEST"
1150 RETURN
1160 REM ************
1170 REM ROOM 3
1180 PRINT "YOU ARE IN THE WRECKED HOLD
OF A SPACESHIP"
1190 PRINT "THE CAVERNOUS INTERIOR IS LI
TTERED WITH"
1200 PRINT "FLOATING WRECKAGE, AS IF FRO
M SOME"
1205 PRINT "TERRIBLE EXPLOSION EONS AGO.
....."
1210 RETURN
1220 REM ************
1230 REM ROOM 4
1240 IF RND>.6 THEN PRINT "WHAT A SUPERB
 SIGHT......"
1242 PRINT "THE VIEW OF THE STARS FROM T
HIS OBSERVATION"
1245 PRINT "PLATFORM IS MAGNIFICENT, AS
FAR AS THE EYE"
```

```
1246 PRINT "CAN SEE. THE SINGLE EXIT IS
BACK WHERE YOU"
1250 PRINT "CAME FROM"
1260 RETURN
1270 REM ************
1280 REM ROOM 5
1290 PRINT "ACRE UPON ACRE OF DRIED-UP H
YDROPONIC"
1300 PRINT "PLANT BEDS STRETCH AROUND YO
U. ONCE THIS"
1310 PRINT "AREA FED THE THOUSAND ON BOA
RD THE SHIP"
1320 IF RND>.5 THEN PRINT "THE SOLAR LAM
PS ARE STILL SHINING"
1330 IF RND>.5 THEN PRINT "A FEW PLANTS
ARE STILL ALIVE TO THE EAST"
1340 RETURN
1350 REM ************
1360 REM ROOM 6
1370 PRINT "YOU ARE FREE. YOU HAVE MADE
IT. YOUR"
1380 PRINT "POD SAILS FREE INTO SPACE...
........"
1385 PRINT "YOUR SCORE WAS";3*TALLY + 5*
STRENGTH + 2*WEALTH + 10*OXY + 30*MK
1390 END
1400 REM ************
1410 REM ROOM 7
1420 PRINT "YOU ARE IN THE CREW'S SLEEPI
NG QUARTERS"
1430 IF RND >.5 THEN PRINT "MOST OF THE
SLEEPING SHELLS ARE EMPTY"
1440 IF RND >.5 THEN PRINT "THE FEW REMA
INING CREW STIR FITFULLY":PRINT "IN THEI
R ENDLESS, DREAMLESS SLEEP"
1445 IF RND>.7 THEN PRINT "THERE ARE EXI
TS TO THE NORTH, EAST AND WEST"
1450 RETURN
1460 REM **************
1470 REM ROOM 8
1480 PRINT "THE FORMER PASSENGER SUSPEND
ED ANIMATION DORMITORY..."
1490 IF RND>.5 THEN PRINT "PASSENGERS FL
OAT BY AT RANDOM"
```

```
1500 IF RND>.5 THEN PRINT "IT IS ENORMOU
S, IT SEEMS TO GO ON FOREVER"
1510 IF RND>.9 THEN PRINT "THE ONLY EXIT
S ARE TO THE WEST AND SOUTH"
1520 RETURN
1530 REM ***************
1540 REM ROOM 9
1550 PRINT "THIS IS THE SHIP'S HOSPITAL,
 WHITE AND STERILE."
1560 PRINT "A BUZZING SOUND, AND A STRAN
GE WARMTH COME FROM"
1570 PRINT "THE SOUTH, WHILE A CHILL IS
FELT TO THE NORTH"
1600 RETURN
1610 REM ***************************
1620 REM ROOM 10
1630 PRINT "FOOD FOR ALL THE CREW WAS PR
EPARED IN THIS"
1640 PRINT "GALLEY. THE REMAINS FROM PRE
PARATIONS OF"
1650 PRINT "FINAL MEAL CAN BE SEEN. DOOR
S LEAVE THE"
1660 PRINT "GALLEY TO THE SOUTH AND TO T
HE WEST"
1680 RETURN
1690 REM *****************
1700 REM ROOM 11
1701 PRINT "AHA...THAT LOOKS LIKE THE SP
ACE POD"
1702 PRINT "NOW, AND ITS OUTSIDE DIALS"
1703 PRINT "INDICATE IT IS STILL IN PERF
ECT CONDITION."
1710 RETURN
1720 REM ****************
1730 REM ROOM 12
1740 IF RND>.5 THEN PRINT "THIS IS THE S
HIP'S MAIN NAVIGATION ROOM"
1750 PRINT "STRANGE MACHINERY LINES THE
WALLS, WHILE"
1760 PRINT "OVERHEAD, A HOLOGRAPHIC STAR
 MAP SLOWLY TURNS"
1765 PRINT "BY THE FLICKERING GREEN LIGH
T YOU CAN JUST"
1766 PRINT "MAKE OUT EXITS":IF RND>.8 TH
```

```
EN PRINT "TO THE SOUTH AND TO THE EAST"
1770 RETURN
1780 REM *****************
1790 REM ROOM 13
1800 IF RND>.5 THEN PRINT "YOUR BODY TWI
STS AND BURNS..."
1810 PRINT "YOU ARE CAUGHT IN A DEADLY R
ADIATION FIELD"
1820 PRINT "SLOWLY YOU REALISE THIS IS T
HE END"
1830 IF RND>.5 THEN PRINT "NO MATTER WHA
T YOU DO"
1835 IF RND>.5 THEN PRINT "YOU ARE DOOME
D TO DIE HERE"
1840 RETURN
1850 REM *****************
1860 REM ROOM 14
1870 PRINT "THIS IS THE POWER CENTER OF
THE SHIP"
1880 PRINT "THE CHARACTERISTIC BLUE META
L LIGHT"
1890 PRINT "OF THE STILL-FUNCTIONING ION
 DRIVE"
1900 PRINT "FILLS THE ENGINE ROOM. THROU
GH THE"
1910 PRINT "HAZE YOU CAN SEE DOORS"
1920 IF RND>.9 THEN PRINT "TO THE NORTH
AND WEST"
1930 IF RND>.6 THEN PRINT "A SHAFT LEADS
 DOWNWARDS TO THE REPAIR CENTER"
1940 RETURN
1950 REM ****************
1960 REM ROOM 15
1970 PRINT "YOU ARE STANDING IN THE ANDR
OID STORAGE HOLD"
1980 PRINT "ROW UPON ROW OF METAL MEN ST
AND STIFFLY AT"
1990 PRINT "ATTENTION, AWAITING THE DIST
INCTIVE SOUND OF"
2000 PRINT "THEIR LONG-DEAD CAPTAIN TO S
ET THEM INTO MOTION"
2010 PRINT "A LIGHT COMES FROM THE WEST
AND THROUGH THE"
2015 PRINT "GRAVITY WELL SET INTO THE FL
```

```
OOR"
2016 RETURN
2020 REM *****************
2030 REM ROOM 16
2040 PRINT "ANOTHER CAVERNOUS, SEEMINGLY
 ENDLESS HOLD,"
2050 PRINT "THIS ONE CRAMMED WITH GOODS
FOR TRADING..."
2060 IF RND>.7 THEN PRINT "RARE METALS A
ND VENUSIAN SCULPTURES"
2065 IF RND>.8 THEN PRINT "PRESERVED SCA
LAPIAN DESERT FISH"
2066 IF RND>.7 THEN PRINT "FLASHING EBON
Y SCITH STONES FROM XARIAX IV"
2067 IF RND>.8 THEN PRINT "AWESOME TRADE
R ANT EFIGIES FROM THE QWERTYIOPIAN EMPI
RE"
2070 IF RND>.9 THEN PRINT "THE LIGHT IS
STRONGER TO THE WEST"
2080 RETURN
2090 REM ***************
2100 REM ROOM 17
2110 PRINT "A STARK, METALLIC ROOM, REEK
ING OF LUBRICANTS"
2120 PRINT "WEAPONS LINE THE WALL, RANK
UPON RANK. EXITS FOR"
2130 PRINT "SOLDIER ANDROIDS ARE TO THE
NORTH AND THE EAST"
2140 RETURN
2150 REM ****************
2160 REM ROOM 18
2170 PRINT "ABOVE YOU IS THE GRAVITY SHA
FT LEADING TO"
2180 PRINT "THE ENGINE ROOM. THIS IS THE
 SHIP REPAIR"
2190 PRINT "CENTER WITH EMERGENCY EXITS
TO THE SOLDIER"
2200 PRINT "ANDROIDS STORAGE AND TO THE
TRADING GOODS HOLD"
2210 RETURN
2220 REM **************
2230 REM ROOM 19
2240 PRINT "YOU'VE STUMBLED ON THE SECRE
T COMMAND CENTER"
```

```
2250 PRINT "WHERE SCREENS BRING VIEWS FR
OM ALL AROUND"
2260 PRINT "THE SHIP. THERE ARE TWO EXIT
S........"
2270 IF RND>.5 THEN PRINT "ONE OF WHICH
IS THE GRAVITY WELL" ELSE PRINT "ONE OF
WHICH LEADS TO THE GOODS HOLD"
2280 RETURN
2290 REM ***************
2300 REM DEAD END
2310 PRINT "YOU HAVE RUN OUT OF OXYGEN..
.."
2320 GOSUB 3520
2330 GOTO 1385
2340 REM ***************
2350 REM PICK UP TREASURE
2360 IF A(RO,7)<10 THEN PRINT "THERE IS
NOTHING OF VALUE HERE":GOSUB 3520:RETURN

2370 IF LIGHT=0 THEN PRINT "YOU CANNOT S
EE WHERE IT IS":GOSUB 3520:RETURN
2380 WEALTH=WEALTH + A(RO,7)
2390 A(RO,7)=0
2400 RETURN
2410 REM ***************
2420 REM UNSUCCESSFUL ATTEMPT TO RUN
2430 PRINT "NO YOU MUST STAND AND FIGHT"

2440 A$="F"
2450 GOSUB 3520
2460 GOTO 620
2470 REM ***************
2480 REM REPLENISH OXYGEN
2490 CLS
2500 IF OXY<1 THEN RETURN
2510 PRINT "YOU HAVE";OXY;"UNITS OF OXYG
EN LEFT"
2520 PRINT "HOW MANY DO YOU WANT TO ADD
TO YOUR TANKS";
2530 INPUT Z
2540 IF Z>OXY THEN 2530
2550 OXY=INT(OXY-Z)
2560 STRENGTH=INT(STRENGTH+5*Z)
2570 GOSUB 3410:CLS
```

```
2580 RETURN
2590 REM ***********
2600 REM INITIALISE
2610 CLS
2620 STRENGTH=INT(RND(1)*50) + 75
2630 WEALTH=INT(RND(1)*50) + 50
2640 OXY=INT(RND(1)*16)
2650 TALLY=0
2655 QQ=0
2660 MK=0:REM NO. OF ANDROIDS/ALIENS DES
TROYED
2670 REM **************
2680 REM SET UP SPACE SHIP
2690 DIM A(19,7)
2700 FOR B=1 TO 19
2710 FOR C=1 TO 7
2720 READ A(B,C)
2730 NEXT C
2740 NEXT B
2750 INPUT "WHAT IS YOUR NAME, SPACE HER
O";N$
2760 CLS
2770 RO=3:REM STARTING POSITION (RO=ROOM
 NUMBER)
2780 LASER=0
2790 TRANSPORTER=0
2800 ION=0
2810 SUIT=0
2820 LIGHT=0
2830 REM **************
2840 REM ALLOT VALUABLES
2850 FOR J = 1 TO 7
2860 M=INT(RND(1)*19)+1
2870 IF M=6 OR M=11 OR RO=13 OR A(M,7)<>
0 THEN 2860
2880 A(M,7)=INT(RND(1)*100)+10
2890 NEXT J
2900 REM **************
2910 REM ALLOT ALIENS/ANDROIDS
2915 FOR T=1 TO 2
2920 FOR J = 1 TO 4
2930 M=INT(RND(1)*18)+1
2940 IF M=6 OR M=11 OR M=13 OR A(M,7)<>0
 THEN 2930
```

```
2950 A(M,7)= -J
2960 NEXT J
2965 NEXT T
2990 RETURN
3000 REM ******************************
3010 REM SUPPLY ANDROID
3020 PRINT "A SUPPLY ANDROID HAS ARRIVED
"
3030 GOSUB 3260
3040 IF WEALTH<.1 THEN Z=0:GOTO 3130
3050 PRINT "YOU CAN BUY 1 - NUCLEONIC LI
GHT ($15)"
3060 PRINT "            2 - ION GUN ($10
)"
3070 PRINT "            3 - LASER ($20)"

3080 PRINT "            4 - OXYGEN ($2 P
ER UNIT)"
3090 PRINT "            5 - MATTER TRANS
PORTER ($30)"
3100 PRINT "            6 - COMBAT SUIT
($50)"
3110 PRINT "            0 - TO CONTINUE
EXPLORATION"
3120 INPUT "ENTER NO. OF ITEM REQUIRED";
Z
3130 IF Z=0 THEN CLS:RETURN
3140 IF Z=1 THEN LIGHT=1:WEALTH=WEALTH-1
5
3150 IF Z=2 THEN ION=1:WEALTH=WEALTH-10
3160 IF Z=3 THEN LASER=1:WEALTH=WEALTH-2
0
3170 IF Z=5 THEN TRANSPORTER=1:WEALTH=WE
ALTH-30
3180 IF Z=6 THEN SUIT=1:WEALTH=WEALTH-50

3190 IF WEALTH<0 THEN PRINT "YOU HAVE TR
IED TO CHEAT ME!":WEALTH=0:SUIT=0:LIGHT=
0:ION=0:LASER=0:TRANSPORTER=0:OXY=INT(OX
Y/4):GOSUB 3520
3200 IF Z<>4 THEN 3030
3210 INPUT "HOW MANY UNITS OF OXYGEN";Q:
Q=INT(Q)
3220 IF 2*Q>WEALTH THEN PRINT "YOU HAVEN
```

```
'T GOT ENOUGH MONEY":GOTO 3210
3230 OXY=OXY+Q
3240 WEALTH=WEALTH-2*Q
3250 GOTO 3030
3260 IF WEALTH>0 THEN PRINT:PRINT:PRINT
"YOU HAVE $";WEALTH;"IN SOLARIAN CREDITS
"
3270 IF WEALTH=0 THEN PRINT "YOU HAVE NO
 SOLARIAN CREDITS LEFT":GOSUB 3520:RETUR
N
3280 FOR J=1 TO 4:PRINT:NEXT J
3290 RETURN
3300 REM *******************
3310 DATA 0,5,2,0,0,0,0:REM ROOM 1
3320 DATA 0,0,0,1,0,0,0:REM ROOM 2
3330 DATA 3,7,4,3,3,3,0:REM ROOM 3
3340 DATA 0,0,0,3,0,0,0:REM ROOM 4
3350 DATA 1,5,7,5,5,5,0:REM ROOM 5
3360 DATA 6,6,6,6,6,6,0: REM ROOM 6
3370 DATA 3,0,8,5,0,0,0: REM ROOM 7
3380 DATA 8,12,8,7,8,8,0: REM ROOM 8
3390 DATA 11,13,10,0,0,0,0:REM ROOM 9
3400 DATA 0,14,0,9,0,0,0:REM ROOM 10
3410 DATA 9,6,6,6,6,6,0:REM ROOM 11
3420 DATA 8,16,19,0,0,0,0:REM ROOM 12
3430 DATA 13,0,0,13,0,13,0:REM ROOM 13
3440 DATA 10,0,15,17,0,18,0:REM ROOM 14
3450 DATA 0,0,0,14,0,19,0:REM ROOM 15
3460 DATA 12,16,16,18,16,16,0:REM ROOM 1
6
3470 DATA 14,0,18,0,0,0,0:REM ROOM 17
3480 DATA 0,0,16,17,14,0,0:REM ROOM 18
3490 DATA 0,12,0,0,15,0,0:REM ROOM 19
3500 REM *******************
3510 REM ADJUST LOOP BELOW TO YOUR SYSTE
M
3520 FOR T=1 TO 900:NEXT T
3530 RETURN
```

18

TRICKS AND TRAPS

I hope you have entered the Asimovian Disaster program, and attempted to solve it before coming to this chapter. You will gain far more from this book by doing so, rather than just reading on, without actually entering the material as you come to it.

The Map

First of all, the map is far more complex than was the castle map:

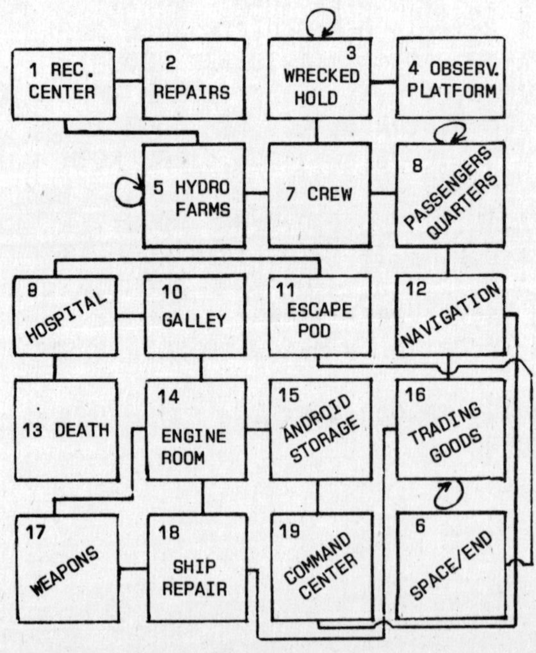

There are several unusual things about this map, things you should include in your own, hard-to-solve Adventure programs.

For a start, some of the rooms (3, 5, 8, and 16) have "endless loop" exits which leave you where you started. This is a useful technique if you want to give the impression of size. All these rooms, as you'll see if you check the map, are large rooms which could quite conceivably stretch for a long, long way. The hydroponic farms (room 5) could cover acres, and the hold (room 3) where you start, along with the hold which contains goods for trading (room 16), could be almost as big.

The other room (room 8) contains over 1,000 passengers so it must be fairly large.

You should use this "endless loop" idea in two situations. The first is when you want something to appear very big ("YOU ARE IN A DESERT WHICH STRETCHES FOR MILES IN EVERY DIRECTION"). The second situation is when you want to trap the player in a maze, which has only one way out, which may well be the uttering of a magic word or the bribing of a dwarfling rather than finding a hidden exit.

What Goes Up

To further confuse players, you can have rooms connected by tunnels which do not connect them from expected directions (as could happen within a massive spaceship or in an underground labyrinth). To try and explain what I mean by this, look at rooms 14 and 17. To go from 14 to 17 you leave to the west, but you leave to the north from room 17 to get back to 14.

The situation is even more confusing with rooms 15, 19, and 16 (and further compounded by 16's endless loop). You go down from 15 to reach 19 (and up from 19 to get back to 15) but south from 19 to enter 12 from the west. Figuring that one out could take an Adventurer many hours.

Room of Death

If you make the wrong decision in the hospital (room 9) you end up in room 13, which is not a room at all, but "death by radiation." As you'll see if you trace the way "room 13" is used, spare rooms like this can be very convenient as ways of storing special deaths for the player.

One-Way System

Although all connections in this game are two-way (a situation which does not have to occur) you'll see by looking carefully at the map that the player can end up in some pretty dead ends. Room 2, for example, forces the player to retrace his or her steps all the way back to room 7, before any real progress can be made. Room 4, the observation platform, provides nothing but a look at the stars (which, if nothing else, helps set the atmosphere of the Adventure).

The only way to get to the room where you'll find your Escape Pod is via one or more of the rooms at the bottom of the map, and—as we've discussed earlier—there are a number of confusing traps in this section.

Adding It All Up

By studying this Adventure, and especially the map and its corresponding Travel Table held in the DATA statements, you'll learn a lot about ways of making your Adventures harder to solve, while still keeping to the rule regarding a coherent environment.

Roll Your Own

You've seen how easy it is to modify a given listing to produce an Adventure program which appears totally original. You could now go back to the very first WEREWOLVES AND WANDERER and draw up a map of your own, in the setting of a scenario which you've thought of, and write an Adventure program of your own. As you can see from THE ASIMOVIAN DISASTER, much of the work has already been done for you.

19

THE CITADEL OF PERSHU

Our next program, the biggest in the book so far, occupies around 18K. THE CITADEL OF PERSHU pits you against a fantastic array of monsters and assorted deviant entities. It has more than 40 rooms and the action takes place on three different levels.

This program brings together all the ideas we've discussed so far for Adventure programs, and adds a number of new ones, such as the ability to carry objects and to drop them in rooms (and discover, wonder of wonders, that they are still there when the room is revisited).

The fights are less under the control of the random number generator, and you more or less control the "attributes" (your characteristics within the Adventure) with which you will fight. If you don't like the odds at the beginning of a melee, you can even invoke magic spells (you have three per game) which guarantee that you'll win that particular battle.

This is emphatically not an easy Adventure to solve. There are a number of tricks and traps within it, not all of which I will explain to you. It seems to me to make much more sense to throw you straight into the Adventure, and let you encounter (and eventually solve) the problems presented to you. Examining the relevant part of the listing after you've solved the problem will fairly quickly reveal how the problem was encoded into the program, and investigating this will show you how to include such puzzles within your own Adventure programs.

The Vocabulary

Many Adventure programs, as I pointed out earlier, appear to cater to very wide vocabularies. This program, like the ones which precede it, accepts only a limited set of words, and needs these as single letter input.

This is satisfactory for the time being, although you'll probably be interested to know that when we get to our next program, the last one in the book, we will be using a form of input which allows the computer to accept, and understand, two-word commands, like GET AXE, SLAY DRAGON, and DROP DIAMOND.

However, the emphasis in this program, apart from being designed to act as a teaching tool, is on ease of playing, so that the player can concentrate on deciphering the map, and on getting to the end of the apparently endless maze of rooms, stairways, and passages.

Therefore, nearly all inputs are taken in the form of INKEY$, so you do not need to press RETURN after entering a command. Here is the standard vocabulary, and apart from entering a number when confronted with a menu of choices from time to time, this vocabulary is all you will need (enter just the first letter):

Quit
Fight
Run (away from a fight; rarely successful)
Pick up (there is only one object in a room, so it knows which one you mean)
Get rid of (you can only drop something you are carrying which you indicate from a menu, and you cannot drop something if there is already an object in the room; monsters do not count as objects)
North
South
East
West
Up
Down

Snapshots

This apparently small vocabulary allows you a surprising degree of choice in many situations, as you can see from these "snapshots" of THE CITADEL OF PERSHU in action:

```
ANDREW
MAGIC SPELLS: YOU HAVE 3 LEFT
YOU HAVE             $ 100
```

```
STRENGTH: 12    CHARISMA: 9
DEXTERITY: 3    INTELLIGENCE: 3
WISDOM: 12    CONSTITUTION: 18

THIS IS THE ENTRANCE TO THE CITADEL OF PERSHU
TURN NOW, IF YOU WISH. MANY STRONGER THAN YOU
HAVE TAKEN FRIGHT AT ITS MENACING TOWERS AND
DARK PORTALS. IF YOU WISH TO PROCEED, MOVE
EAST TOWARDS THE BLACK, GAPING DOORWAY...

YOU CAN SEE....
FLAMING TORCH

WHAT DO YOU WANT TO DO? P
```

```
ANDREW
MAGIC SPELLS: YOU HAVE 3 LEFT
YOU HAVE FLAMING TORCH              $ 100

STRENGTH: 12    CHARISMA: 9
DEXTERITY: 3    INTELLIGENCE: 3
WISDOM: 12    CONSTITUTION: 18

A STONE ALTAR STANDS IN THE MIDDLE OF THE ROOM
WITH TWO DEAD CANDLES ON IT. AN OLD BOOK LIES
ON ONE PART OF THE ALTAR TOP, AND A FADED, RED
PARCHMENT CLOTH COVERS THE FRONT OF IT

YOU CAN SEE....
CHAIN MAIL ARMOR

WHAT DO YOU WANT TO DO? P
```

Later in the same game. . . .

```
ANDREW
MAGIC SPELLS: YOU HAVE 3 LEFT
YOU HAVE FLAMING TORCH SILVER KEY
         CHAIN MAIL ARMOR     $ 310
STRENGTH: 12    CHARISMA: 9
DEXTERITY: 3    INTELLIGENCE: 3
WISDOM: 12    CONSTITUTION: 18

YOU ARE IN THE RULER'S BEDCHAMBER
A LARGE FIRE BURNS IN THE SOUTH OF


THE ROOM, WITH A SMALL DOOR BESIDE
IT. OTHER EXITS ARE TO THE NORTH
AND TO THE WEST

THE ROOM CONTAINS A MAGI
WITH ATTRIBUTES AS FOLLOWS:
STRENGTH: 15   CHARISMA: 12
DEXTERITY: 18   INTELLIGENCE: 6
WISDOM: 9   CONSTITUTION: 15

WHAT DO YOU WANT TO DO? F

YOUR ATTRIBUTES ARE:
1 - STRENGTH 12     2 - CHARISMA 9
3 - DEXTERITY 3   4 - INTELLIGENCE 3
5 - WISDOM 12       6 - CONSTITUTION 18

CHAIN MAIL ARMOR GIVES YOU AN EDGE
ENTER 1 TO FIGHT WITH MAGIC
OR 2 TO RELY ON SKILL? 2

WHICH ATTRIBUTES TO FIGHT WITH (2)? 5,6
```

```
YOU WOUND THE MAGI
YOU HAVE KILLED THE MAGI
______________________________________
```

Still later. . . .

```
ANDREW
MAGIC SPELLS: YOU HAVE 3 LEFT
MONSTERS KILLED: 2
YOU HAVE FLAMING TORCH              $ 100

STRENGTH: 2    CHARISMA: 17
DEXTERITY: 3    INTELLIGENCE: 18

WISDOM: 5    CONSTITUTION: 2

YOU ARE IN THE CENTRAL, CIRCULAR
AREA OF THE WINE CELLAR. THERE IS
A DOOR AT EACH COMPASS POINT.

THE ROOM CONTAINS A HELL HOUND
WITH ATTRIBUTES AS FOLLOWS:
STRENGTH: 12   CHARISMA: 6
DEXTERITY: 15   INTELLIGENCE: 18
WISDOM: 6   CONSTITUTION: 9

WHAT DO YOU WANT TO DO? F


ENTER 1 TO FIGHT WITH MAGIC
OR 2 TO RELY ON SKILL? 2

WHICH ATTRIBUTES TO FIGHT WITH (2)? 4,2

THE FIGHT STARTS IN FAVOR OF YOU
THE HELL HOUND - 24
ANDREW - 35
```

```
YOU WOUND THE HELL HOUND
THE HELL HOUND - 23
ANDREW - 35

YOU WOUND THE HELL HOUND
THE HELL HOUND - 22
ANDREW - 35

YOU GET IN A GLANCING BLOW
THE HELL HOUND - 21
ANDREW - 35

YOU ARE WOUNDED!!
YOU HAVE KILLED THE HELL HOUND
```

And finally. . .

```
THE FLAMES STRIKE AT YOU...
AS YOU SLOWLY BURN TO DEATH

YOUR FINAL SCORE, ANDREW, IS 1145
YOU COMPLETED 13 % OF THE QUEST
```

Attributes

As you can see from the above, you are blessed with six characteristics in this game:

STRENGTH—raw muscle power
INTELLIGENCE—raw brain-power
CHARISMA—personal magnetism
WISDOM—brain-power tempered by experience
DEXTERITY—ability with weapons
CONSTITUTION—stamina

Due to the strange workings of the world within which this Adventure takes place, every entity you meet (from the PHASE SPI-

DER and HYDRA OF 10 HEADS to the FIRE LIZARD and NECROMANCER) has exactly the same characteristics. However, you only have to fight with two of them. If you are wise, you will choose the two in which you most exceed the enemy. You battle it out based on the total of the two chosen attributes, modified to some extent (in your favor) by the weapons (SWORD or WAR HAMMER), protective devices (CHAIN MAIL ARMOR, SHIELD, CLOAK OF PROTECTION), and all-purpose thingy (WAND OF FIREBALLS).

Don't worry if this seems complex. It should all be perfectly clear when you actually run the program. Once you examine the relevant part of the program (lines 3690 to 4190), you'll see how the attributes are used to set up the background for the fight, and how they are modified while the fight is in progress. Note that a serious defeat can kill you, at which point the program terminates abruptly.

The Goodies

There are many treasures lying around the Citadel. Although you can pick these up (and the more wealth you have at the end of the game, the better your final score), you cannot drop them. When you pick them up, their value is added to your wealth, and they cease to exist in any other form.

The treasures you'll find around the Citadel, with different values each time you play the game, are:

EMERALDS	PIECES OF EIGHT
SILVER RINGS	ELEMENTAL GEMS
ELVEN AMYTHESTS	SHAPE-SHIFTING STONES
DIAMOND DRAGON EYES	GOLD DUBLOONS
A CRYSTAL BALL	

As well as the nine treasures above, there are nine objects (mentioned a short while ago) which you may come across during the game, and these you may pick up (and, if you choose, put down). The nine objects are:

A FLAMING TORCH	CHAIN MAIL ARMOR
SILVER KEY	SHIELD
GOLD KEY	CLOAK OF PROTECTION
SWORD	WAND OF FIREBALLS
WAR HAMMER	

The two keys are important. There are two locked doors in the Adventure, which bar you from discovering further parts of the map.

You cannot get past these doors without the relevant keys. The first locked door needs the silver key (the first key you'll find) and the second one (right near the end of the Adventure) demands the gold one. The keys effectively vanish from your possession after they have been used, as they stay in their relevant doors. They can't be used for anything else anyway.

You are utterly lost without the torch, so you must pick it up the moment you see it. Without it (as you'll discover if you put it down in a room, when it is immediately extinguished!) you won't be able to see anything. (If you do want to experiment by putting the torch down, you'll be pleased to discover that it automatically relights itself when picked up.)

Picking things up from rooms, and placing objects there adds another dimension of "reality" to an Adventure environment, as you'll discover. Dropping something in one room, wandering about for a while, and then returning and finding it still there is (to my humble mind, anyway) quite exciting, as it adds another degree of solidity to the world you have created and are experiencing.

Be warned, this is a pretty weird map. The "store rooms" are a labyrinth of seven interconnected rooms, and you must work your way through them to get to the exit which, after all, is the point of the program.

The wine cellar is a miracle of modern architecture. It consists of a central, circular area, with a room at each compass point. A tunnel connects the north door of the northern room with the west door of the western room.

As you can see from these two rooms alone, working out the map is not going to be easy.

Multiple Choice Death

The program actually allows for 47 rooms, rather than the 43 which are on the map. The final four "rooms" are for rather dramatic deaths. When you think about it, you can see that a death is, more or less, "entered" from a room, especially when you fall into a fire, or step in a swiftly flowing stream which bears you away to a watery grave. The dramatic deaths which are disguised as rooms in this Adventure are as follows:

Room 44—death by drowning
Room 45—death by burning
Room 46—freezing forever into living stone by magic
Room 47—death by falling into a bottomless pit

You can easily incorporate deaths into your own programs in this way. Allowing people to tumble to their deaths from high towers, or to stumble down bottomless pits when the room is so filled with smoke they cannot see properly (as happens in this Adventure) is a good way of keeping the tension level high.

Incidents like these deaths, along with the extremely complex (but still consistent and stable) map, ensure that your friends will not easily solve this Adventure. You're going to have enough problems yourself, especially if you do not cheat, and do not look at the map before you try and work it out yourself.

The Baddies

Your problems will be compounded by the enemies you'll have to confront within the Citadel. Those you meet will be chosen from the following list (and they, like the treasure, will be in different locations each time you run the program): SWASHBUCKLER, WEREBEAR, CAECLIAE, MANTICORE, VAMPIRE, PREDEBEAST, GARGOYLE, MEDUSAE, MAGI, FIRE LIZARD, PHASE SPIDER, TROLL, HELL HOUND, FROST GIANT, NECROMANCER, HYDRA OF 10 HEADS, PATRIACH, MASTER THIEF, and LIVING STATUE.

Compressing the Program

As you'll see when you examine the complete listing (occupying, as I said, around 18K on my system, an IBM PC, and demanding around two and a half K working space) in the next chapter, it is well supported with REM statements. To save time, you can drop any REM statement which is a row of asterisks (these serve as visual markers, and these line numbers are not called by GOSUBs), as well as any REM statement which follows a line. Do not get rid of REM statements which stand alone, as these are nearly always called by a GOSUB.

Another way of compressing the program is to get rid of all but the first line of description of a room. The PRINT statements, as you'll soon see, take up a massive portion of the room. If you replace a line like REM ROOM 1 with a terse description such as UNDERGROUND RIVER:RETURN, you can then get rid of all the lines which follow the REM in the original listing, up to and including the terminating RETURN.

If you do this to squeeze the program into limited memory, make sure the ON . . . GOSUB calls (lines 470 to 520) actually still do reference the relevant brief descriptions. (If you like, you can provide players with cards which contain the rest of the description, so they can read the information you are unable to fit into your computer. If you do this, you should label the rooms in some way—such as A1, A2, and so on—to make it easy for the player to find the relevant card without undue delay.)

The Maps

Finally, here is the map of the Citadel. I suggest you do not look at it until after you have attempted to solve the Adventure using your own brains. Then, by all means, come back to it in this book, and compare it with your own map. This comparison, and a close inspection of how the program achieves its various ends will serve as an excellent illustration for our discussions on creating Adventure games.

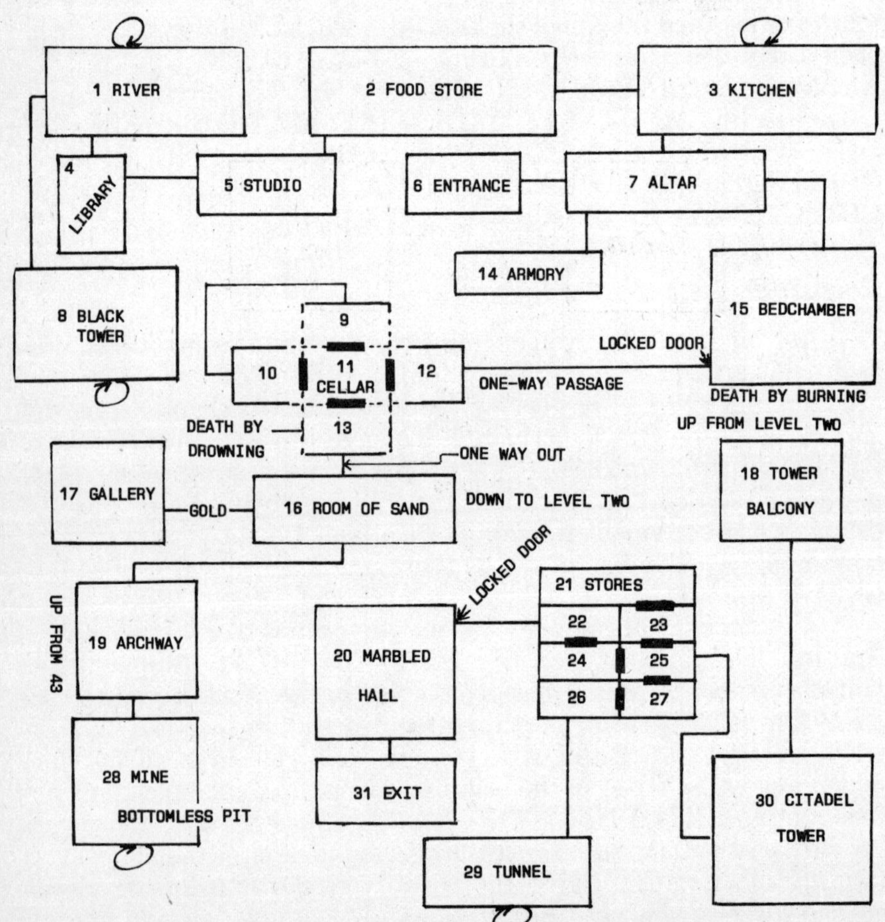

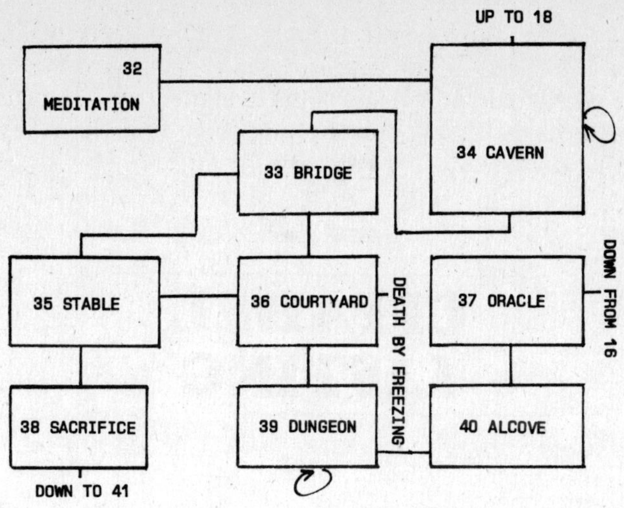
UP TO 18
32
MEDITATION
33 BRIDGE
34 CAVERN
35 STABLE
36 COURTYARD
DEATH BY FREEZING
37 ORACLE
DOWN FROM 16
38 SACRIFICE
39 DUNGEON
40 ALCOVE
DOWN TO 41

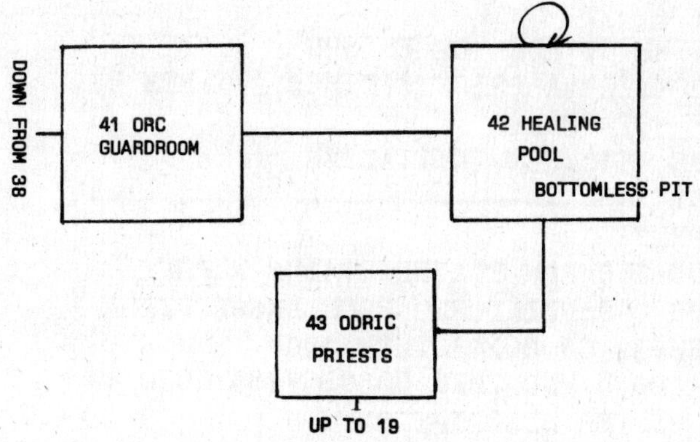
DOWN FROM 38
41 ORC
GUARDROOM
42 HEALING
POOL
BOTTOMLESS PIT
43 ODRIC
PRIESTS
UP TO 19

20

CITADEL LISTING

This chapter contains the entire CITADEL listing:

```
10 REM THE CITADEL OF PERSHU
20 RANDOMIZE VAL(RIGHT$(TIME$,2)):REM DE
LETE IF NOT NEEDED
30 GOSUB 4510:REM INITIALISE
40 PRINT "-----------------------------------
----":PRINT
50 GOSUB 260:REM PLAYER STATUS REPORT
60 GOSUB 440:PRINT:REM ROOM DESCRIPTION
70 IF RO=31 OR RO>43 THEN 190
80 IF A(RO,8)<>0 THEN GOSUB 3180:GOTO 11
0:REM MONSTER DESCRIPTION
90 IF RO=6 AND LI=0 THEN GOSUB 3340:REM
TO GET TORCH
100 IF A(RO,7)<>0 AND LI=1 THEN GOSUB 33
40:REM CONTENTS DESCRIPTION
110 GOSUB 4210:REM ACCEPT PLAYER COMMAND

120 IF ST*CH*DE*IN*WI*CO=0 THEN 170
130 TALLY=TALLY+1
140 IF RO=15 THEN C(2)=0
150 IF RO=20 THEN C(3)=0
160 GOTO 40
170 PRINT "YOUR COMBINED ATTRIBUTES ARE
NO LONGER"
```

```
180 PRINT "ENOUGH TO SUSTAIN YOU...YOU A
RE DEAD!"
190 PRINT:PRINT "YOUR FINAL SCORE, ";N$"
, IS";
200 PRINT 3*CASH + 30*MK + 3*(ST+CH+DE+I
N+WI+CO) + TALLY
210 W=RO+TALLY/1000:IF W>99 THEN W=W-RND
(1)*8:GOTO 210
220 IF RO=31 THEN W=100
230 PRINT "YOU COMPLETED";INT(W);"% OF T
HE QUEST"
240 END
250 REM ********************
260 REM PLAYER STATUS REPORT
270 PRINT N$
280 IF M>0 THEN PRINT "MAGIC SPELLS: YOU
 HAVE";M;"LEFT"
290 IF MK>0 THEN PRINT "MONSTERS KILLED:
";MK
300 PRINT "YOU HAVE ";
310 FOR J=1 TO 9:PRINT T$(C(J));" ";:NEX
T J
320 IF CASH>0 THEN PRINT "$";CASH
330 IF ST<0 THEN ST=0
340 IF CH<0 THEN CH=0
350 IF DE<0 THEN DE=0
360 IF IN<0 THEN IN=0
370 IF WI<0 THEN WI=0
380 IF CO<0 THEN CO=0
390 PRINT:PRINT "STRENGTH:";ST;"   CHARI
SMA:";CH
400 PRINT "DEXTERITY:";DE;"   INTELLIGEN
CE:";IN
410 PRINT "WISDOM:";WI;"   CONSTITUTION:
";CO:PRINT
420 RETURN
430 REM ***************
440 REM ROOM DESCRIPTION
450 IF LI=0 AND RO<>6 THEN PRINT "IT IS
VERY DARK":GOSUB 5430:RETURN
460 IF RO> 19 THEN 490
470 ON RO GOSUB 550,600,650,710,760,810,
880,940,1000,1070,1140,1190,1260,1330,13
70,1440,1530,1610,1660
```

```
480 GOSUB 5430:RETURN
490 IF RO>35 THEN 520
500 Z=RO-19:ON Z GOSUB 1710,1770,1820,18
60,1900,1940,1970,2010,2050,2120,2180,22
10,2260,2320,2360,2420
510 GOSUB 5430:RETURN
520 Z=RO-35:ON Z GOSUB 2460,2520,2590,26
50,2720,2760,2810,2850,2920,2990,3060,31
10
530 GOSUB 5430:RETURN
540 REM ****************************
550 REM ROOM 1
560 PRINT "AN UNDERGROUND RIVER FLOWS SW
IFTLY BY"
570 IF RND(1)>.5 THEN PRINT "THERE IS AN
 EXIT TO THE WEST"
580 IF RND(1)>.5 THEN PRINT "A TUNNEL LE
ADS TO THE SOUTH"
590 RETURN
600 REM ROOM 2
610 PRINT "YOU ARE IN THE CITADEL'S FOOD
 STORAGE AREA"
620 PRINT "OLD CHEESES AND BLACK LOAVES
OF BREAD CAN"
630 PRINT "BE SEEN, AS WELL AS MANY SACK
S OF SUPPLIES"
640 RETURN
650 REM ROOM 3
660 PRINT "YOU ARE IN THE CITADEL'S KITC
HEN. A HUGE"
670 PRINT "JOINT OF MEAT TURNS SLOWLY OV
ER A RAGING"
680 PRINT "FIRE. DOORS LEAD INTO CUPBOAR
DS, AS WELL"
690 PRINT "AS TO THE WEST AND TO THE SOU
TH"
700 RETURN
710 REM ROOM 4
720 PRINT "THIS IS THE CENTRAL LIBRARY.
LEATHER-BOUND"
730 PRINT "VOLUMES LINE THE WALLS, RIGHT
 UP TO THE"
740 PRINT "ORNATELY-CARVED CEILING..."
750 RETURN
```

```
760 REM ROOM 5
770 PRINT "THIS ROOM IS AN AWFUL MESS. I
T USED TO"
780 PRINT "AN ARTIST'S STUDIO. PAINT AND
 OLD"
790 PRINT "EASELS LIE AROUND THE FLOOR"
800 RETURN
810 REM ROOM 6
820 PRINT "THIS IS THE ENTRANCE TO THE C
ITADEL OF PERSHU"
830 PRINT "TURN NOW, IF YOU WISH. MANY S
TRONGER THAN YOU"
840 PRINT "HAVE TAKEN FRIGHT AT ITS MENA
CING TOWERS AND"
850 PRINT "DARK PORTALS. IF YOU WISH TO
PROCEED, MOVE"
860 PRINT "EAST TOWARDS THE BLACK, GAPIN
G DOORWAY..."
870 RETURN
880 REM ROOM 7
890 PRINT "A STONE ALTAR STANDS IN THE M
IDDLE OF THE ROOM"
900 PRINT "WITH TWO DEAD CANDLES ON IT.
AN OLD BOOK LIES"
910 PRINT "ON ONE PART OF THE ALTAR TOP,
 AND A FADED, RED"
920 PRINT "PARCHMENT CLOTH COVERS THE FR
ONT OF IT"
930 RETURN
940 REM ROOM 8
950 PRINT "YOU STAND HIGH ON THE BLACK T
OWER, THE"
960 PRINT "CITADEL STRETCHES TO THE NORT
H, SOUTH"
970 PRINT "AND EAST OF YOU."
980 PRINT "THERE IS ONLY ONE WAY OUT"
990 RETURN
1000 REM ROOM 9
1010 PRINT "YOU ARE IN THE NORTHERN SECT
ION OF THE"
1020 PRINT "CITADEL'S LARGE WINE CELLAR.
 HEAVY"
1030 PRINT "BARRELS LIE ALL AROUND YOU I
N THIS END"
```

```
1040 PRINT "OF THE CELLAR. THERE IS A DO
OR TO THE NORTH"
1050 PRINT "AND ONE TO THE SOUTH"
1060 RETURN
1070 REM ROOM 10
1080 PRINT "YOU ARE IN THE WEST WING OF
THE WINE"
1090 PRINT "CELLAR. THERE IS A DOOR TO T
HE WEST AND"
1100 PRINT "ONE TO THE EAST. THE CENTRAL
, CIRCULAR"
1110 PRINT "PART OF THE CELLAR LIES BEYO
ND THE"
1120 PRINT "EAST DOOR."
1130 RETURN
1140 REM ROOM 11
1150 PRINT "YOU ARE IN THE CENTRAL, CIRC
ULAR"
1160 PRINT "AREA OF THE WINE CELLAR. THE
RE IS"
1170 PRINT "A DOOR AT EACH COMPASS POINT
."
1180 RETURN
1190 REM ROOM 12
1200 PRINT "YOU ARE IN THE EAST SECTION
OF THE"
1210 PRINT "WINE CELLAR. THERE IS A DOOR
 TO THE"
1220 PRINT "WEST AND ONE - WHICH YOU CAN
NOT USE,"
1230 PRINT "AS IT ONLY ALLOWS ENTRANCE T
O WHERE"
1240 PRINT "YOU NOW STAND - TO THE EAST"

1250 RETURN
1260 REM ROOM 13
1270 PRINT "THERE ARE MANY, MANY WINE BO
TTLES HERE"
1280 PRINT "LYING ON THEIR SIDES, IN THI
S SOUTHERN"
1290 PRINT "SECTION OF THE WINE CELLAR.
THERE IS A"
1300 PRINT "DARK, UNFRIENDLY-LOOKING HOL
E TO THE WEST"
```

```
1310 PRINT "AND DOORS TO THE NORTH AND T
O THE SOUTH"
1320 RETURN
1330 REM ROOM 14
1340 PRINT "THIS IS THE CITADEL'S ARMORY
. ROW UPON ROW"
1350 PRINT "OF SHINY SUITS OF ARMOR ARE
STORED HERE..."
1360 RETURN
1370 REM ROOM 15
1380 PRINT "YOU ARE IN THE RULER'S BEDCH
AMBER"
1390 PRINT "A LARGE FIRE BURNS IN THE SO
UTH OF"
1400 PRINT "THE ROOM, WITH A SMALL DOOR
BESIDE"
1410 PRINT "IT. OTHER EXITS ARE TO THE N
ORTH"
1420 PRINT "AND TO THE WEST"
1430 RETURN
1440 REM ROOM 16
1450 PRINT "THIS CURIOUS ROOM HAS A FLOO
R COVERED"
1460 PRINT "IN SAND, HEAPED ALL OVER THE
 PLACE"
1470 PRINT "BY PEEPING OVER THE 'DUNES'
YOU CAN"
1480 PRINT "SEE A GOLDEN PASSAGEWAY LEAD
S TO THE"
1490 PRINT "WEST, AND THERE IS A DOOR TO
 THE SOUTH"
1500 PRINT "YOU ARE NOT SURE WHETHER OR
NOT YOU"
1510 PRINT "HAVE SEEN ALL THE EXITS":RET
URN
1520 RETURN
1530 REM ROOM 17
1540 PRINT "YOU ARE IN THE PICTURE GALLE
RY. PORTRAITS"
1550 PRINT "OF LONG-DEAD PRINCES LINE AL
L OF THE"
1560 PRINT "WALLS. THE ROOM IS DOMINATED
 BY A HUGE"
1570 PRINT "LANDSCAPE, HANGING ABOVE THE
```

```
 EXIT TO THE"
1580 PRINT "EAST WHICH LEADS, VIA THE GO
LD PASSAGEWAY"
1590 PRINT "BACK TO THAT CURIOUS ROOM OF
 SAND"
1600 RETURN
1610 REM ROOM 18
1620 PRINT "YOU ARE ON A REMOTE TOWER BA
LCONY"
1630 IF RND(1)>.5 THEN PRINT "A BAT FLIE
S PAST YOU, SHRIEKING"
1640 PRINT "THERE ARE STAIRS HERE"
1650 RETURN
1660 REM ROOM 19
1670 PRINT "YOU WALK BENEATH A STONE ARC
HWAY"
1680 PRINT "YOU CAN ONLY WALK NORTH OR S
OUTH"
1690 PRINT "UNLESS YOU DECIDE TO TAKE TH
E STAIRS"
1700 RETURN
1710 REM ROOM 20
1720 PRINT "THIS VAST HALL HAS A MARBLE
FLOOR, AND"
1730 PRINT "THE SLIGHTEST SOUND ECHOES V
IOLENTLY"
1740 PRINT "THERE ARE PURPLE DRAPES CONC
EALING"
1750 PRINT "THE EXITS FROM THIS HALL"
1760 RETURN
1770 REM ROOM 21
1780 PRINT "YOU ARE IN THE GLOVE STORERO
OM"
1790 PRINT "THE WEST DOOR RADIATES HEAT"

1800 PRINT "ANOTHER DOOR LEADS TO THE SO
UTH"
1810 RETURN
1820 REM ROOM 22
1830 PRINT "YOU ARE IN THE SILVER CROSSE
S STOREROOM"
1840 PRINT "THERE ARE ONLY TWO EXITS"
1850 RETURN
1860 REM ROOM 23
```

```
1870 PRINT "YOU ARE IN THE AMULET STORER
OOM"
1880 PRINT "DOORS LEAD NORTH, AND SOUTH"

1890 RETURN
1900 REM ROOM 24
1910 PRINT "YOU ARE IN THE KAZOO STORERO
OM"
1920 PRINT "THERE ARE TWO EXITS"
1930 RETURN
1940 REM ROOM 25
1950 PRINT "YOU ARE IN THE SATCHEL STORE
ROOM"
1960 RETURN
1970 REM ROOM 26
1980 PRINT "YOU ARE IN THE STOREROOM FOR
 WOODEN"
1990 PRINT "BOXES...THERE ARE TWO EXITS"

2000 RETURN
2010 REM ROOM 27
2020 PRINT "THIS IS WHERE PRINTED VASES
ARE"
2030 PRINT "STORED...AS YOU CAN EASILY S
EE"
2040 RETURN
2050 REM ROOM 28
2060 PRINT "THE HEAVY AIR OF THIS AREA S
EEMS TO MAKE"
2070 PRINT "YOUR TORCH VERY DIM. YOU CAN
 HARDLY SEE"
2080 PRINT "AIR IS RUSHING UP FROM SOMEW
HERE"
2090 PRINT "YOU CAN JUST MAKE OUT THAT T
HIS AREA MUST"
2100 PRINT "DE A MINE OF SOME SORT"
2110 RETURN
2120 REM ROOM 29
2130 PRINT "YOU APPEAR TO BE IN AN ENDLE
SS LABYRINTH,"
2140 PRINT "LINED WITH PAINTINGS.......
."
2150 PRINT "WHICHEVER WAY YOU TURN, THER
E SEEMS TO"
```

```
2160 PRINT "BE MORE TUNNELS, ALL LINED W
ITH PAINTINGS"
2170 RETURN
2180 REM ROOM 30
2190 PRINT "THIS IS THE SOUTHERN TOWER O
F THE CITADEL"
2200 RETURN
2210 REM ROOM 31
2220 PRINT "WELL DONE, YOU HAVE MANAGED
TO FIND THE"
2230 PRINT "THE EXIT. TAKE A DEEP BREATH
 OF GOOD,"
2240 PRINT "CLEAN AIR.........."
2250 RETURN
2260 REM ROOM 32
2270 PRINT "THIS ROOM IS FILLED WITH SWI
RLING SMOKE"
2280 PRINT "SO YOU CANNOT SEE...AIR RUSH
ES PAST A"
2290 PRINT "STATUE OF THE GODDESS DIANA.
 THIS"
2300 PRINT "MUST BE THE CITADEL'S MEDITA
TION CHAMBER"
2310 RETURN
2320 REM ROOM 33
2330 PRINT "A SMALL FORKED BRIDGE CROSSE
S A STREAM"
2340 PRINT "HERE. YOU CAN MOVE NORTH, SO
UTH OR WEST"
2350 RETURN
2360 REM ROOM 34
2370 PRINT "YOU ARE IN A ROUGH STONE CAV
ERN, WITH"
2380 PRINT "STAIRS LEADING UP FROM IT"
2390 PRINT "THERE IS ALSO A SINGLE DOOR
WHICH"
2400 PRINT "LEADS AWAY FROM THE CAVERN"
2410 RETURN
2420 REM ROOM 35
2430 PRINT "THIS IS THE FORMER CITADEL U
NDERGROUND"
2440 PRINT "STABLE. IT SMELLS TERRIBLE"
2450 RETURN
2460 REM ROOM 36
```

```
2470 PRINT "YOU FIND YOURSELF IN AN UNDE
RGROUND"
2480 PRINT "COURTYARD. STRANGE, TWISTED
TREES ARE"
2490 PRINT "AROUND YOU, AND A WIND OF IN
CREDIBLE"
2500 PRINT "COLDNESS BLOWS FROM THE EAST
"
2510 RETURN
2520 REM ROOM 37
2530 PRINT "THIS IS THE ORACLE ROOM, ALT
HOUGH THE"
2540 PRINT "MYSTIC VOICE HAS NOT SPOKEN
FOR MANY"
2550 PRINT "YEARS"
2560 IF RND(1)>.3 THEN PRINT "BUT NOW IT
 TELLS YOU THERE IS":PRINT "A HIDDEN STA
IRWELL IN THE ROOM"
2570 IF RND(1) >.7 THEN PRINT "THE VOICE
 FAINTLY MURMURS OF THE DOOR TO THE SOUT
H"
2580 RETURN
2590 REM ROOM 38
2600 PRINT "HORRORS. A COLD SHUDDER PASS
ES THROUGH AS YOU"
2610 PRINT "REALISE THIS IS THE PRIESTS'
 SACRIFICE ROOM"
2620 PRINT "DRIED UP BLOOD IS ON THE FLO
OR, AND AN"
2630 PRINT "SKULL GRINS AT YOU, FROM HIG
H ON THE WALL"
2640 RETURN
2650 REM ROOM 39
2660 PRINT "OLD STRAW MATTRESSES, AND RI
NGS CHAINED TO THE"
2670 PRINT "WALL TELL YOU THIS WAS THE C
ITADEL'S DUNGEON"
2680 IF RND(1)>.4 THEN PRINT "A SMALL DO
OR LEADS TO THE NORTH":PRINT "AND ANOTHE
R TO THE EAST"
2690 PRINT "THE DUNGEON SEEMS TO STRETCH
 FOREVER, WITH MANY"
2700 PRINT "SMALL PARTITIONED AREAS...."
2710 RETURN
```

```
2720 REM ROOM 40
2730 PRINT "YOU ARE IN A SMALL ALCOVE, W
ITH A SOLID"
2740 PRINT "GREY GRANITE THRONE IN THE M
IDDLE OF IT"
2750 RETURN
2760 REM ROOM 41
2770 PRINT "THIS IS THE ORC'S GUARDROOM,
 WAY BELOW"
2780 PRINT "THE GROUND. A STAIRWELL ENDS
 HERE, AND"
2790 PRINT "A DOOR LEADS TO THE EAST"
2800 RETURN
2810 REM ROOM 42
2820 PRINT "THERE IS A HEALING POOL HERE
, WITH A"
2830 PRINT "DANGEROUS, SWIRLING AREA OF
WATER"
2840 RETURN
2850 REM ROOM 43
2860 PRINT "THE UNDERPRIESTS OF ODRIC US
ED THIS"
2870 PRINT "TINY HALL FOR THEIR FORBIDDE
N WORSHIP"
2880 PRINT "EONS AGO. IT IS AN UNPLEASAN
T AREA,"
2890 PRINT "SO YOU ARE THRILLED TO SEE A
 SET OF"
2900 PRINT "STONE STAIRS"
2910 RETURN
2920 REM ROOM 44, DEATH BY DROWNING
2930 PRINT "WATER COVERS YOUR HEAD"
2940 GOSUB 5430
2950 PRINT "YOU ARE DROWNING"
2960 GOSUB 5430
2970 PRINT "GLUG...GASP..............."
2980 RETURN
2990 REM ROOM 45, DEATH BY BURNING
3000 PRINT "THE FLAMES STRIKE AT YOU..."

3010 GOSUB 5430
3020 PRINT "AS YOU SLOWLY BURN TO DEATH"

3030 GOSUB 5430
```

```
3040 IF RND(1)>.7 THEN 3000
3050 RETURN
3060 REM ROOM 46, FREEZING
3070 PRINT "YOU ARE HIT BY A FREEZING SP
ELL"
3080 PRINT "AND TURN INTO A BLOCK OF PER
PETUAL"
3090 PRINT "LIVING STONE. THIS IS THE EN
D"
3100 RETURN
3110 REM ROOM 47, BOTTOMLESS PIT
3120 PRINT "YOU TUMBLE DOWN A BOTTOMLESS
 PIT"
3130 GOSUB 5430
3140 PRINT "DOWN, DOWN, DOWN..."
3150 IF RND(1)>.4 THEN 3130
3160 RETURN
3170 REM ********************
3180 REM MONSTER DESCRIPTION
3190 G$=M$(A(RO,8))
3200 S1=(INT(RND(1)*6)+1)*3
3210 H1=(INT(RND(1)*6)+1)*3
3220 D1=(INT(RND(1)*6)+1)*3
3230 I1=(INT(RND(1)*6)+1)*3
3240 W1=(INT(RND(1)*6)+1)*3
3250 C1=(INT(RND(1)*6)+1)*3
3260 IF RND(1)>.5 THEN PRINT "YOU COME F
ACE TO FACE WITH A ";G$ ELSE PRINT "THE
ROOM CONTAINS A ";G$
3270 PRINT "WITH ATTRIBUTES AS FOLLOWS:"

3280 PRINT "STRENGTH:";S1;"  CHARISMA:";
H1
3290 PRINT "DEXTERITY:";D1;"  INTELLIGEN
CE:";I1
3300 PRINT "WISDOM:";W1;"  CONSTITUTION:
";C1
3310 GOSUB 5430
3320 RETURN
3330 REM ********************
3340 REM CONTENTS DESCRIPTION
3350 G$=T$(A(RO,7))
3360 VALUE=INT(RND(1)*100)+56
3370 PRINT "YOU CAN SEE...."
```

```
3380 GOSUB 5430
3390 PRINT G$
3400 IF A(RO,7)>9 THEN PRINT "WORTH $";V
ALUE
3410 GOSUB 5430
3420 RETURN
3430 REM ************************
3440 REM PICK UP TREASURE
3450 IF LI=0 AND A(RO,7)<>1 THEN PRINT "
IT IS TOO DARK TO SEE ANYTHING":GOSUB 54
30:RETURN
3460 IF A(RO,7)=1 THEN LI=1:REM PLAYER I
S CARRYING LIGHT
3470 IF A(RO,7)>9 THEN CASH=CASH+VALUE:G
OTO 3490
3480 C(A(RO,7))=A(RO,7)
3490 A(RO,7)=0
3500 RETURN
3510 REM ***********************
3520 REM GET RID OF OBJECTS
3530 FLAG=0
3540 FOR Z=1 TO 9:IF C(Z)<>0 THEN FLAG=1

3550 NEXT Z
3560 IF FLAG=0 THEN PRINT "YOU HAVE NOTH
ING TO GET RID OF":GOSUB 5430:RETURN
3570 IF A(RO,7)<>0 THEN PRINT "THERE IS
ALREADY SOMETHING HERE":GOSUB 5430:RETUR
N
3580 PRINT "YOU ARE CARRYING:"
3590 FOR Z=1 TO 9
3600 IF C(Z)<>0 THEN PRINT Z;" ";T$(Z)
3610 NEXT Z
3620 PRINT:INPUT "ENTER NUMBER OF OBJECT
 TO DROP";K
3630 IF C(K)=0 THEN PRINT "YOU ARE NOT C
ARRYING ";T$(K):GOSUB 5430:GOTO 3620
3640 IF K=1 THEN LI=0:REM TURN LIGHT OFF

3650 A(RO,7)=K
3660 C(K)=0
3670 RETURN
3680 REM ************************
3690 REM THE BIG FIGHT
```

```
3700 IF A(RO,8)=0 THEN RETURN
3710 PRINT:PRINT "YOUR OPPONENT IS A ";G
$
3720 MT=0:HT=0:REM MONSTER TALLY, HUMAN
TALLY
3730 PRINT "WITH THE FOLLOWING ATTRIBUTE
S:"
3740 PRINT "1 - STRENGTH";S1;"   2 - CHA
RISMA";H1
3750 PRINT "3 - DEXTERITY";D1;"  4 - INT
ELLIGENCE";I1
3760 PRINT "5 - WISDOM";W1;"     6 - CON
STITUTION";C1
3770 PRINT:PRINT "YOUR ATTRIBUTES ARE:"
3780 PRINT "1 - STRENGTH";ST;"   2 - CHA
RISMA";CH
3790 PRINT "3 - DEXTERITY";DE;"  4 - INT
ELLIGENCE";IN
3800 PRINT "5 - WISDOM";WI;"     6 - CON
STITUTION";CO
3810 PRINT:IF C(4)<> 0 THEN PRINT "YOU H
AVE A SWORD":HT=HT+1
3820 IF C(5)<>0 THEN PRINT "YOUR WAR HAM
MER WILL BE OF AID":HT=HT+1
3830 IF C(6)<>0 THEN PRINT "CHAIN MAIL A
RMOR GIVES YOU AN EDGE":HT=HT+1
3840 IF C(7)<>0 THEN PRINT "YOUR SHIELD
WILL HELP IN THIS FIGHT":PRINT "AGAINST
THE ";G$:HT=HT+1
3850 IF C(8)<>0 THEN PRINT "THE CLOAK OF
 PROTECTION SURROUNDS YOU":HT=HT+1
3860 IF C(9)<>0 THEN PRINT "THE WAND OF
FIREBALLS ENHANCES YOUR STRENGTH":HT=HT+
1
3870 IF M>0 THEN PRINT "ENTER 1 TO FIGHT
 WITH MAGIC":INPUT "OR 2 TO RELY ON SKIL
L";Q:IF Q<1 OR Q>2 THEN 3870
3880 IF M>0 AND Q=1 THEN M=M-1:PRINT "YO
UR MAGIC DESTROYS IT":GOSUB 5430:MK=MK+1
:GOTO 4190
3890 PRINT:INPUT "WHICH ATTRIBUTES TO FI
GHT WITH (2)";Z,Q
3900 IF Z<1 OR Q<1 OR Z>6 OR Q>6 OR Z=Q
THEN PRINT "NO CHEATING!":GOTO 3890
```

```
3910 IF Z=1 OR Q=1 THEN MT=MT+S1:HT=HT+S
T
3920 IF Z=2 OR Q=2 THEN MT=MT+H1:HT=HT+C
H
3930 IF Z=3 OR Q=3 THEN MT=MT+D1:HT=HT+D
E
3940 IF Z=4 OR Q=4 THEN MT=MT+I1:HT=HT+I
N
3950 IF Z=5 OR Q=5 THEN MT=MT+W1:HT=HT+W
I
3960 IF Z=6 OR Q=6 THEN MT=MT+C1:HT=HT+C
O
3970 PRINT:PRINT "THE FIGHT STARTS IN FA
VOR OF ";
3980 IF HT>MT THEN PRINT "YOU" ELSE PRIN
T "THE ";G$
3990 K=INT(RND(1)*8)
4000 PRINT "THE ";G$;" -";MT
4010 PRINT N$;" -";HT:PRINT
4020 IF K=0 THEN PRINT "YOU GET IN A GLA
NCING BLOW":MT=MT-1
4030 IF K=1 THEN PRINT "THE ";G$;" STRIK
ES OUT!":HT=HT-3:ST=ST-1:CH=CH-1
4040 IF K=2 THEN PRINT "YOU DRAW THE ";G
$;"'S BLOOD":MT=MT-1
4050 IF K=3 THEN PRINT "YOU ARE WOUNDED!
!":HT=HT-(INT(RND(1)*3)+1):DE=DE-1
4060 IF K=4 THEN PRINT "THE ";G$;" IS TI
RING":MT=MT-1
4070 IF K=5 THEN PRINT "YOU ARE BLEEDING
....":HT=HT-2:WI=WI-1:CO=CO-1
4080 IF K=6 THEN PRINT "YOU WOUND THE ";
G$:MT=MT-1
4090 IF K=7 THEN K=INT(RND(1)*CASH + 1):
PRINT "IT KNOCKS $";K;" FROM YOUR HAND":
CASH=CASH-K
4100 IF RND(1)>.25 AND HT>0 AND MT>0 THE
N FOR T=1 TO 1600:NEXT T:GOTO 3990
4110 IF HT>MT THEN PRINT "YOU HAVE KILLE
D THE ";G$:MK=MK+1:GOTO 4190
4120 PRINT "THE ";G$;" GOT THE BETTER OF
 YOU THAT TIME"
4130 IF Z=1 OR Q=1 THEN ST=4*INT(ST/5)
4140 IF Z=2 OR Q=2 THEN CH=3*INT(CH/4)
```

```
4150 IF Z=3 OR Q=3 THEN DE=6*INT(DE/7)
4160 IF Z=4 OR Q=4 THEN IN=2*INT(IN/3)
4170 IF Z=5 OR Q=5 THEN WI=5*INT(WI/6)
4180 IF Z=6 OR Q=6 THEN CO=3*INT(CO/6)
4190 A(RO,8)=0:GOSUB 5430:RETURN
4200 REM ***********************
4210 REM ACCEPT PLAYER COMMAND
4220 IF INKEY$<>"" THEN 4220
4230 PRINT:PRINT "WHAT DO YOU WANT TO DO
?":PRINT
4240 Z$=INKEY$
4250 IF Z$="" THEN 4240
4260 IF Z$="Q" THEN PRINT "COWARD...QUIT
TER....TURNCOAT...":GOTO 190
4270 IF Z$="F" AND A(RO,8)=0 THEN PRINT
"THERE IS NOTHING TO FIGHT":GOTO 4220
4280 IF Z$="F" THEN GOSUB 3690
4290 IF Z$="P" AND A(RO,7)=0 THEN PRINT
"THERE IS NOTHING TO PICK UP":GOTO 4220
4300 IF Z$="G" THEN GOSUB 3520
4310 IF Z$="R" AND RND(1)>.4 AND A(RO,8)
<>0 THEN PRINT "NO, YOU MUST STAND AND F
IGHT":Z$="F"
4320 IF Z$="R" THEN INPUT "WHICH DIRECTI
ON WILL YOU RUN";Z$
4330 IF Z$="P" THEN GOSUB 3440
4340 IF Z$="F" THEN GOSUB 3690
4350 IF Z$="N" AND A(RO,1)=0 THEN PRINT
"NO EXIT THAT WAY":GOTO 4220
4360 IF Z$="S" AND A(RO,2)=0 THEN PRINT
"THERE IS NO EXIT SOUTH":GOTO 4220
4370 IF Z$="E" AND A(RO,3)=0 THEN PRINT
"YOU CANNOT GO IN THAT DIRECTION":GOTO 4
220
4380 IF Z$="W" AND A(RO,4)=0 THEN PRINT
"YOU CANNOT MOVE THROUGH SOLID STONE":GO
TO 4220
4390 IF Z$="U" AND A(RO,5)=0 THEN PRINT
"THERE IS NO WAY UP FROM HERE":GOTO 4220

4400 IF Z$="D" AND A(RO,6)=0 THEN PRINT
"YOU CANNOT DESCEND FROM HERE":GOTO 4220
4410 IF RO=15 AND C(2)=0 AND Z$="E" THEN
 PRINT "YOU NEED THE SILVER KEY TO UNLOC
```

```
K THE DOOR":GOTO 4220
4420 IF RO=22 AND C(3)=0 AND Z$="W" THEN
 PRINT "YOU NEED THE GOLD KEY TO UNLOCK
THE DOOR":GOTO 4220
4430 IF Z$="N" THEN RO=A(RO,1)
4440 IF Z$="S" THEN RO=A(RO,2)
4450 IF Z$="E" THEN RO=A(RO,3)
4460 IF Z$="W" THEN RO=A(RO,4)
4470 IF Z$="U" THEN RO=A(RO,5)
4480 IF Z$="D" THEN RO=A(RO,6)
4490 RETURN
4500 REM **********
4510 REM INITIALISE
4520 CLS
4530 DIM A(43,8),C(9),T$(18),M$(19)
4540 TALLY=0:LI=0:RO=6:CASH=100:MK=0:M=3

4550 ST=3*(INT(RND(1)*6)+1)
4560 CH=3*(INT(RND(1)*6)+1)
4570 DE=3*(INT(RND(1)*6)+1)
4580 IN=3*(INT(RND(1)*6)+1)
4590 WI=3*(INT(RND(1)*6)+1)
4600 CO=3*(INT(RND(1)*6)+1)
4610 REM ****************
4620 REM ROOM DIRECTIONS
4630 FOR B=1 TO 43
4640 FOR C=1 TO 8
4650 READ A(B,C)
4660 NEXT C:NEXT B
4670 REM *****************
4680 REM ALLOT MONSTERS
4690 FOR J = 1 TO 15
4700 T=INT(RND(1)*43)+1:IF T=6 OR T=31 O
R T=4 OR T=21 THEN 4700
4710 IF A(T,8)<>0 THEN 4700
4720 A(T,8)=J
4730 NEXT J
4740 REM *****************
4750 REM ALLOT TREASURE
4760 FOR J = 4 TO 18
4770 T=INT(RND(1)*43)+1:IF T=6 OR T=31 T
HEN 4770
4780 IF A(T,7)<>0 THEN 4770
4790 A(T,7)=J
```

```
4800 NEXT J
4810 REM ************************
4820 INPUT "WHAT IS YOUR NAME, EXPLORER"
;N$
4830 CLS
4840 REM ******************
4850 REM NAME TREASURES/MONSTERS
4860 FOR J=1 TO 18
4870 READ T$(J)
4880 NEXT J
4890 FOR J=1 TO 19
4900 READ M$(J)
4910 NEXT J
4920 RETURN
4930 REM ***************
4940 DATA 1,4,1,8,0,0,0,0:REM ROOM 1
4950 DATA 0,5,3,0,0,0,0,0:REM ROOM 2
4960 DATA 3,7,3,2,0,0,0,0:REM ROOM 3
4970 DATA 1,0,5,0,0,0,2,0:REM ROOM 4
4980 DATA 2,0,0,4,0,0,0,0:REM ROOM 5
4990 DATA 0,0,7,0,0,0,1,0:REM ROOM 6, EN
TRANCE
5000 DATA 3,14,15,6,0,0,0,0:REM ROOM 7
5010 DATA 1,8,8,8,0,0,0,0:REM ROOM 8
5020 DATA 10,11,0,0,0,0,0,0:REM ROOM 9
5030 DATA 0,0,11,9,0,0,0,0:REM ROOM 10
5040 DATA 9,13,12,10,0,0,0,0:REM ROOM 11
5050 DATA 0,0,0,11,0,0,0,0:REM ROOM 12
5060 DATA 11,16,0,44,0,0,0,0:REM ROOM 13
5070 DATA 7,0,0,0,0,0,0,0:REM ROOM 14
5080 DATA 7,45,0,12,0,0,0,0:REM ROOM 15
5090 DATA 0,19,0,17,0,37,0,0:REM ROOM 16
5100 DATA 0,0,16,0,0,0,0,0:REM ROOM 17
5110 DATA 0,30,0,0,0,34,0,0:REM ROOM 18
5120 DATA 16,28,0,0,0,43,0,0:REM ROOM 19
5130 DATA 0,31,22,0,0,0,0,0:REM ROOM 20
5140 DATA 0,23,0,45,0,0,3,0:REM ROOM 21
5150 DATA 0,24,0,20,0,0,0,0:REM ROOM 22
5160 DATA 21,25,0,0,0,0,0,0:REM ROOM 23
5170 DATA 22,0,25,0,0,0,0,0:REM ROOM 24
5180 DATA 23,27,30,24,0,0,0,0:REM ROOM 2
5
5190 DATA 0,0,27,0,0,0,0,0:REM ROOM 26
5200 DATA 25,0,0,26,0,0,0,0:REM ROOM 27
```

```
5210 DATA 19,28,28,28,0,47,0,0:REM ROOM
28
5220 DATA 26,29,29,29,0,0,0,0:REM ROOM 2
9
5230 DATA 18,0,0,25,0,0,0,0:REM ROOM 30
5240 DATA 20,0,0,0,0,0,0,0:REM ROOM 31
5250 DATA 0,0,34,0,0,47,0,0:REM ROOM 32
5260 DATA 34,36,0,35,0,0,0,0:REM ROOM 33

5270 DATA 34,33,34,32,18,0,0,0:REM ROOM
34
5280 DATA 33,38,36,0,0,0,0,0:REM ROOM 35

5290 DATA 33,39,46,35,0,0,0,0:REM ROOM 3
6
5300 DATA 0,40,0,0,16,0,0,0:REM ROOM 37
5310 DATA 35,0,0,0,0,41,0,0:REM ROOM 38
5320 DATA 36,39,40,39,0,0,0,0:REM ROOM 3
9
5330 DATA 37,0,0,39,0,0,0,0:REM ROOM 40
5340 DATA 0,0,42,0,38,0,0,0:REM ROOM 41
5350 DATA 42,43,42,41,0,47,0,0:REM ROOM
42
5360 DATA 0,0,42,0,19,0,0,0:REM ROOM 43
5370 REM ******************************
5380 REM TREASURE/MONSTERS
5390 DATA "FLAMING TORCH","SILVER KEY","
GOLD KEY","SWORD","WAR HAMMER","CHAIN MA
IL ARMOR","SHIELD","CLOAK OF PROTECTION"
,"WAND OF FIREBALLS"
5400 DATA "EMERALDS","SILVER RINGS","ELV
EN AMYTHESTS","DIAMOND DRAGON EYES","CRY
STAL BALL","PIECES OF EIGHT","ELEMENTAL
GEMS","SHAPE-SHIFTING STONES","GOLD DUBL
OONS"
5410 DATA "SWASHBUCKLER","WEREBEAR","CAE
CLIAE","MANTICORE","VAMPIRE","PREDEBEAST
","GARGOYLE","MEDUSAE","MAGI","FIRE LIZA
RD","PHASE SPIDER"
5420 DATA "TROLL","HELL HOUND","FROST GI
ANT","NECROMANCER","HYDRA OF 10 HEADS","
PATRIACH","MASTER THIEF","LIVING STATUE"

5430 FOR I=1 TO 999:NEXT:RETURN
```

21

THE ANCIENT CHATEAU

With our final Adventure we break new ground.

This program, which is around 26K long, takes place in a deserted medieval castle in France. The name of the castle is real, all else is imaginary.

Puzzles

In the final chapter of the book, we discuss a number of ways you can increase the level of interest in an Adventure. One way is to have puzzles which the player must solve before continuing. In this program, the puzzle concerns a dwarf, who is going to make sure that if you stumble into the room where he lives, you will not be able to leave, unless you manage to hit the one thing that will enable you to continue.

There are two locked doors, with keys a long way away from the relevant rooms, and as you've experienced before, you must have the right key for the right lock.

Two-Word Sentences

The main difference between this Adventure and the others in the book, is that in this one the computer is given the facility of understanding English—or at least appearing to do so.

The computer is programmed to recognize and act on two-word sentences. The two words must be a verb first, followed by a noun. The computer, for example, can understand the instruction GO NORTH (or even RUN NORTH, MOVE NORTH, CLIMB NORTH, or WALK NORTH). You'll find it is far more satisfying to "talk" to your computer in this way than it is to communicate simply by touching a key.

As was pointed out at the start of the book, some of the pleasure of Adventure programs comes from trying to work out which words it will understand, and which it will reject.

All the objects you encounter within the chateau can be manipulated—at least to the extent of being picked up or put down. Some objects (such as the MYSTIC SCROLL) can be read and others can be drunk. As you can tell from this, the vocabulary handling is quite extensive.

Snapshots

Let's see a little bit of it in action, before I describe how it works. Here's the opening frame:

```
You begin this Adventure in a small
wood outside the Chateau...

While out walking one day, you come
across a small, ramshackle shed in
the woods. Entering it, you see a
hole in one corner...an old ladder
leads down from the hole...

Your attributes are:
    Strength - 11   Charisma - 7
    Dexterity - 10   Intelligence - 11
    Wisdom - 9   Constitution - 7
 What do you want to do? GO DOWN
```

As you can see, you have the six attributes you possessed in earlier Adventures. You'll see that these are slowly reduced as you make your moves. You must find the exit from the chateau before any of them is cut right down to zero.

The computer accepts your two-word command GO DOWN and then informs you that there is no way back:

```
As you stumble down the ladder
you fall into the room. The ladder
crashes down behind you...there
is now no way back...
```

```
A small door leads east from
this very cramped room...

Your attributes are:
    Strength - 10   Charisma - 7
    Dexterity - 10   Intelligence - 10
    Wisdom - 9   Constitution - 6

What do you want to do? MOVE EAST
```

Obviously, it is sink or swim from now on. You must find the exit from the chateau, or die within its walls. After you MOVE EAST, you enter the Hall of Mirrors, which not only contains copper pieces, but also that well-known horror, a "Giolla Dacker."

```
You find yourself in a Hall of
Mirrors...and see yourself
reflected a hundred times or
more...Through the bright glare
you can make out doors in all
directions...You notice the
mirrors around the east door
are heavily tarnished...

  YOU CAN SEE COPPER PIECES

  LOOK OUT!
THERE IS A GIOLLA DACKER HERE!

Your attributes are:
    Strength - 10   Charisma - 7
    Dexterity - 10   Intelligence - 10
    Wisdom - 9   Constitution - 6
```

You decide that money comes ahead of conflict in your scale of values:

```
What do you want to do? GET COPPER
```

Having picked up the coins, you decide it is time to flee, so when asked what you want to do, you enter RUN. But the computer will have none of it:

```
You are carrying:
   COPPER PIECES
        Total value - $ 27

What do you want to do? RUN
RUN      IS JUST ONE WORD
   I NEED TWO
```

So you decide to comply, and enter two words:

```
What do you want to do? RUN SOUTH
```

As in the earlier Adventures, you are not stuck permanently with something simply because you have picked it up:

```
The scent of dying flowers fills
this brightly-lit room...

There are two exits from it..

Your attributes are:
   Strength - 7   Charisma - 2
   Dexterity - 8   Intelligence - 7
   Wisdom - 8   Constitution - 5

You are carrying:
   COPPER PIECES
   EBONY RING
   AMULET
        Total value - $ 440

What do you want to do? DROP COPPER
YOU HAVE DROPPED THE COPPER PIECES
```

The computer is quick to reject input it does not understand:

```
A dried-up fountain stands in the
center of this courtyard, which
once held beautiful flowers...but
have long since died...
```

```
Your attributes are:
   Strength - 6   Charisma - 2
   Dexterity - 8   Intelligence - 7
   Wisdom - 8   Constitution - 5

You are carrying:
   EBONY RING
   AMULET
       Total value - $ 413

What do you want to do? FLY EAST
I DON'T UNDERSTAND 'FLY EAST
```

However, it is worth trying new words, because you never know what it will accept:

```
Through the dim mustiness of
this small potting shed you can
see a stairwell...

Your attributes are:
   Strength - 5   Charisma - 2
   Dexterity - 6   Intelligence - 6
   Wisdom - 8   Constitution - 3

You are carrying:
   MACE
   EBONY RING
   AMULET
   MYSTIC SCROLL
       Total value - $ 608

What do you want to do? READ SCROLL
It says 'THE LOCKS NEED SPECIAL KEYS'
```

I am deliberately not going to tell you too much about CHATEAU GAILLARD, because to do so would rob you completely of the pleasure of playing it. You may well work out some of the puzzles while you are typing it in, but others will not be apparent from the listing. Therefore, I'm leaving you pretty much on your own.

However, this book is intended to share ideas with you which will help you create original Adventure games, so a certain amount of explanation is in order.

Vocabulary Handling

The most important idea introduced in this program is the vocabulary handling which, I hope you'll agree, adds a completely new dimension to the program.

```
360 REM INPUT HANDLING
370 KW=0:REM =1 IF WORD UNDERSTOOD

380 FOR Z=1 TO 1000:NEXT Z
390 INPUT "What do you want to do"
;A$
400 IF A$="" THEN 390
410 AS=ASC(A$)
420 IF AS<65 OR AS>90 THEN PRINT T
AB(3);">>> CAPITAL LETTERS, PLEASE
":PRINT:GOTO 390
```

First, the variable KW (which stands for "key word") is set to zero in line 370. If KW becomes equal to one, then the computer has recognized a phrase it can act on. Line 400 accepts the answer to the question "What do you want to do?" and the following line takes the ASCII code of the first letter of the player's answer. If this is not between 65 and 90, then the player is typing in lower-case letters, so the message from line 420—CAPITAL LETTERS, PLEASE—is triggered, and the program returns to line 390 for a new input.

```
430 M=LEN(A$):IF M<7 THEN A$=A$+"
":GOTO 430
440 B$=LEFT$(A$,3)
450 IF B$="HEL" THEN PRINT "NO HEL
P FOR MORTALS IN THIS GAME!":PRINT
"...although reading and drinking"
:PRINT "may help...":GOTO 40
460 IF B$="QUI" THEN QU=4:GOTO 253
0
```

Line 430 sets M equal to the length of the player's input. It cycles through, adding blank spaces, until it is seven characters long. Line

440 then strips off the first three letters. In common with most Adventure programs, only the first three letters of a command must be entered, so WAL will do for WALK, and FIG for FIGHT. Three letters have been found to be sufficient to avoid ambiguity, and it is good to allow the player to simply enter three letters, rather than the whole word, if that is what he or she wants to do.

Line 450 detects the word HELP and gives a cryptic, but useful, reply, then returns to the beginning of the major handling loop in this program.

Line 460 allows the player to QUIT and sends action to the routine which terminates the program, starting at line 2530.

The next section of the program is the most important part of the vocabulary handling routine:

```
470 N=1
480 IF MID$(A$,N,1)=" " THEN C$=MI
D$(A$,N+1,3):IF LEFT$(C$,1)<>" " T
HEN 530 ELSE 500
490 IF N<M THEN N=N+1:GOTO 480
500 IF RND(1)>.5 THEN 520
510 PRINT TAB(6);"BY ITSELF,";A$:P
RINT TAB(6);"CAN'T BE ACTED ON":GO
TO 390
520 PRINT A$;" IS JUST ONE WORD":P
RINT TAB(4);"I NEED TWO":GOTO 390
```

Line 480 goes through the player input, character by character, looking for the first space which it knows should occur between words one and two (as between RUN and EAST, or GET and DIAMOND). Having found it, the computer sets C$ equal to the first three letters of the second word, to go with its B$ which it earlier set equal to the first three letters of the first word. If it finds that the first letter of C$ is not a space (second statement in line 480) it knows the player's input was two words, so goes to line 530 to continue processing the input.

Line 490 continues the scan through the input.

The computer comes to line 500 if the scan through the input finishes, and the gap between two words has not been found, or (where it is sent by the ELSE in line 480) it discovers that the first character of C$ is a space.

The RND in line 500 chooses between two replies to tell the player a new input is needed, and then goes back to get a new input.

```
530 IF RO<>8 AND RO<>34 THEN 560
540 IF B$="STA" OR B$="KIL" OR B$=
"FIG" OR B$="KIC" OR B$="PUN" OR B
$="SLA" OR B$="ATT" THEN KW=1:GOSU
B 1400
550 IF A(RO,7)>98 AND B$<>"UNL" TH
EN PRINT TAB(4);"** The doors are
locked **":GOTO 40
560 IF B$="STA" OR B$="KIL" OR B$=
"FIG" OR B$="KIC" OR B$="PUN" OR B
$="SLA" OR B$="ATT" THEN KW=1:GOSU
B 1400
570 IF B$="GO " OR B$="MOV" OR B$=
"CLI" OR B$="RUN" OR B$="WAL" THEN
 KW=1:GOSUB 740
580 IF B$="TAK" OR B$="GET" OR B$=
"STE" OR B$="LIF" THEN KW=1:GOSUB
950
590 IF B$="DRO" OR B$="PUT" OR B$=
"THR" OR B$="BRE" THEN KW=1:GOSUB
1160
600 IF B$="UNL" THEN KW=1:GOSUB 23
60
610 IF B$="OPE" THEN KW=1:GOSUB 26
60
620 IF B$="REA" THEN KW=1:GOSUB 27
50
630 IF B$="DRI" OR B$="SWA" THEN K
W=1:GOSUB 2870
640 IF B$="BRI" OR B$="PAY" THEN K
W=1:GOSUB 3000
650 IF KW=1 THEN 700
```

Here, now, is the heart of the computer's ability to "understand" the player's wishes. Line 530 checks to see if the player is in room 8 or in room 34, and if not, jumps to line 560. These two rooms are the ones which are locked at the start of the game, and it is important to check to see whether or not they are still locked before the program continues.

Even if the room is locked, it may contain a monster who feels like a fight, and this takes precedence over the need to unlock the door before proceeding. Look carefully at line 540. It allows the following words to be accepted:

```
STA - for STAB
KIL - for KILL
FIG - for FIGHT
KIC - for KICK
PUN - for PUNCH
SLA - for SLAY
ATT - for ATTACK
```

Any one of those will be accepted, and acted upon. You can see that a player who does not know, in advance, which words the computer will accept, should easily find one or two which will allow the machine to carry out his or her wishes.

Line 550 is only acted on if the contents of the room (the seventh element of A array) is a value greater than 98. This means the door is locked. If this is true, and the B$ part of the string does not contain UNL (as in UNLOCK), the computer will just point out that "The doors are locked" and then go back to the start of the major handling routine for a new input.

Line 560 is a repeat of line 540, but this version of it is reached if the player is not in a room with locked (or potentially locked) doors. You'll see, at the end of line 560, that KW (the variable standing, you'll recall, for "key word") is set equal to 1, meaning a word has been recognized. Finding a word meaning "fight" the computer sets KW equal to 1, then goes to the subroutine from line 1400 where the fight takes place.

Line 570 accepts the words for movement, which are GO, MOVE, CLIMB, RUN, and WALK. It goes to the subroutine from 740, where the actual moves between rooms are made.

Line 580 allows the player to pick up things with TAKE, GET, STEAL, and LIFT. The desire to get rid of things is recognized by line 590, which accepts DROP, PUT, THROW, and BREAK (and when it reaches the subroutine from line 1160, prints out a message—such as WITH A CRASH, THE VASE SMASHES AGAINST THE WALL—which is related to the word you chose to use when making your input.

Line 600 is used when you wish to UNLock the door, 610 if you are OPEning something (such as the chests which litter the place), 620 for REAding, 630 for DRInking or SWAllowing, and line 640 for. . . . But I'm not going to tell you. It was hinted at a little earlier, and I'm not going to repeat the hint. Far better that you have the pleasure of working it out for yourself.

You'll recall that there was a section of code which rejected single word inputs. You'll also recall that the variable KW was to be set to 1 if a word the computer could understand was found. If the computer finds, at line 650, that KW equals 1, then it knows all is probably well. If it does not, the next section of code comes into play:

```
660 R=INT(RND(1)*3)
670 IF R=0 THEN PRINT "IT WOULD NO
T BE WISE TO ";A$
680 IF R=1 THEN PRINT "ONLY A FOOL
 WOULD TRY TO ";A$
690 IF R=2 THEN PRINT "I DON'T UND
ERSTAND '";A$
700 FOR Z=1 TO 500:NEXT Z
710 GOTO 40
720 REM * END OF MAJOR HANDLING LO
OP *
```

The player gets to this section if he or she has entered a two-word phrase, but it is not one which the computer can understand. All obscene entries, often the input of very frustrated players, end up here. The computer chooses one of the three replies, each of which uses the phrase entered by the player, echoing back any rude words. After a pause (line 700) the program returns to the beginning of the major handling routine.

All other parts of this program are simply developments of ideas discussed earlier in the book. You will find that, with the knowledge you've gathered so far in your reading, you should have little trouble in working out how each section works.

The full program listing is given in the next chapter. You'll see that rows of asterisks mark off each section, and REM statements introduce the major routines.

The Map

The map is relatively complicated, as you can see. I suggest you try very hard not to look at it, until you've attempted to map the dungeon yourself.

FIRST LEVEL

1
BATTLEMENTS
2
MAGICIANS' ROOM
3
STRAW MATTRESS
4
WOODEN PANELS
5
LIVING STONE DEATH SPELL
29
DEATH IN A TRAP
8
KITCHEN
9
BLACK DRAGON PICTURE
10
LANDING
UP FROM 39
30
PIT OF FLAMES
6
L-SHAPED ROOM
ARCHWAY
7
N
W
E
S
UP TO 28
STONE ARCHWAY
11
12
WHIRLING SMOKE
13
CHARISMA REDUCTION SPELL
14
WHITE MARBLE
DOWN FROM 27
15
RED DRAPES
16
BRIGHT YELLOW
17
FALL FROM LADDER
18
HALL OF MIRRORS
31
POOL OF ACID
19
LONG CORRIDOR
FUNNEL-WEB SPIDER
32
ALCOVE
21
20
TIMBERED CEILING
23
DYING FLOWERS
22
COURTYARD
CAVERN
24
GAMES ROOM
25
26
POTTING SHED
DOWN TO 33
UP FROM 11
END
28
DOWN TO 17
RAMSHACKLE SHED (START)
27

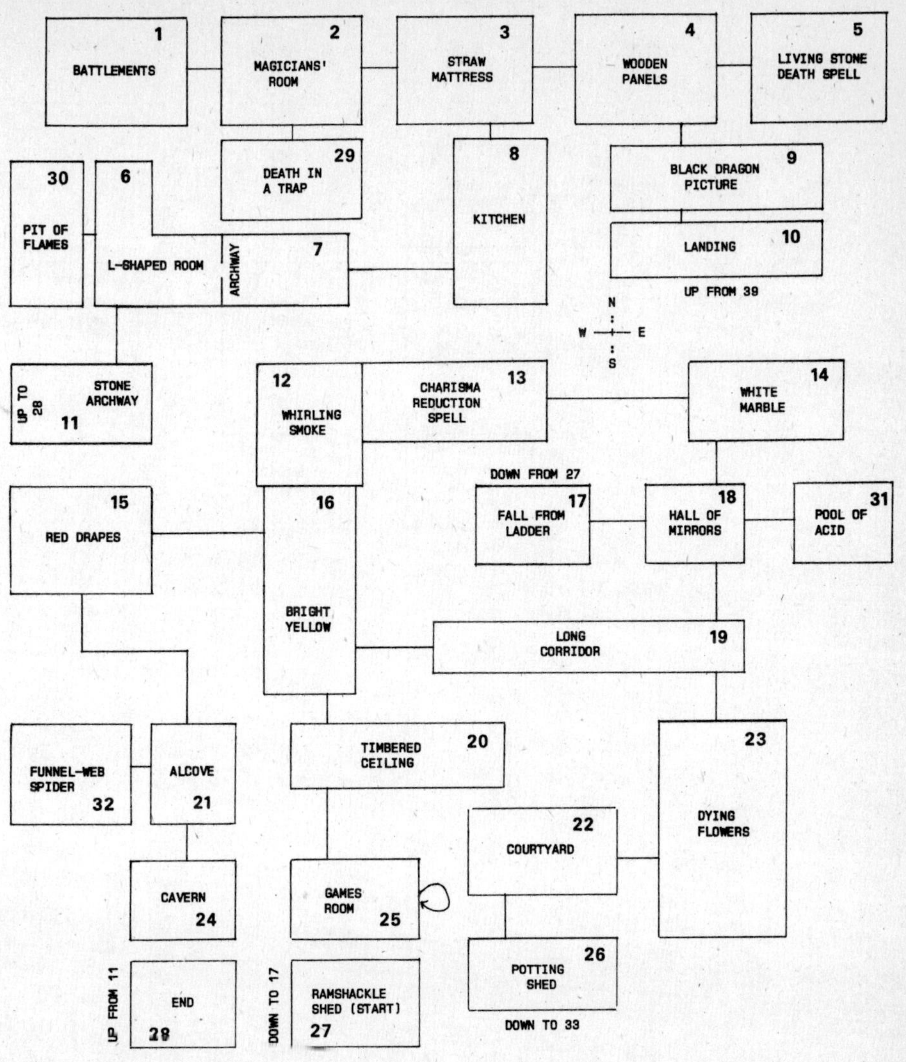

SECOND LEVEL

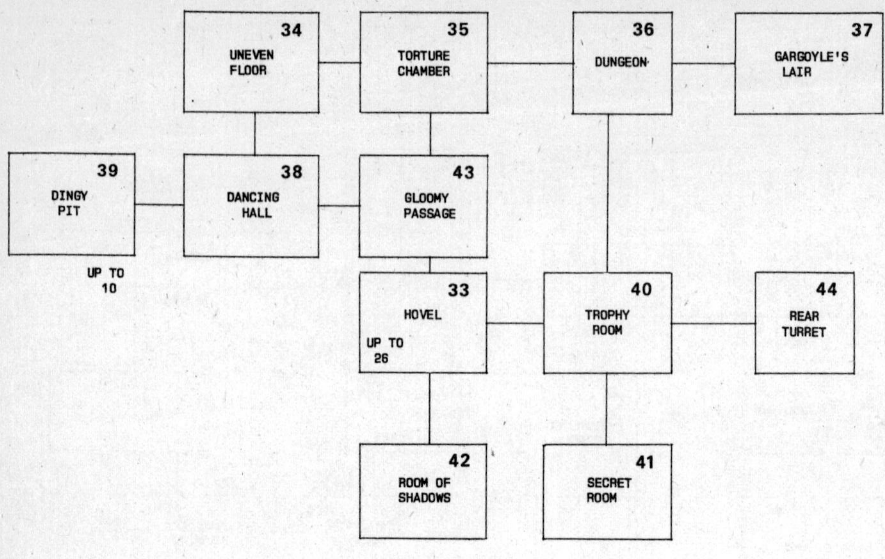

22

CHATEAU LISTING

This chapter contains the full listing of CHATEAU GAILLARD.

```
10 REM CHATEAU GAILLARD
20 GOSUB 6800:REM INITIALISE
30 REM *****************
40 REM REPORT TO PLAYER
50 FOR Z=1 TO 1000:NEXT Z
60 CLS
70 GOSUB 3300:REM ROOM DESCRIPTIONS
80 IF A(RO,7)<>0 OR A(RO,9)<>0 OR A(RO,10)
<>0 THEN GOSUB 6660:REM OBJECTS
90 IF A(RO,7)>98 THEN PRINT "One of the do
ors is locked":PRINT "preventing you from
exploring":PRINT "further"
100 IF A(RO,8)<>0 THEN PRINT TAB(3);"LOOK
OUT!":PRINT "THERE IS A ";M$(A(RO,8));" HE
RE!":IF RND(1)>.7 AND A(RO,8)<>1 THEN PRIN
T "THE ";M$(A(RO,8));" ATTACKS!":KW=1:GOSU
B 1400:GOTO 40
110 IF ST<1 THEN ST=0 ELSE IF RND(1)>.84 T
HEN ST=ST-1
120 IF CH<1 THEN CH=0 ELSE IF RND(1)>.84 T
HEN CH=CH-1
130 IF DE<1 THEN DE=0 ELSE IF RND(1)>.84 T
HEN DE=DE-1
```

```
140 IF IT<1 THEN IT=0 ELSE IF RND(1)>.84 T
HEN IT=IT-1
150 IF WI<1 THEN WI=0 ELSE IF RND(1)>.84 T
HEN WI=WI-1
160 IF CO<1 THEN CO=0 ELSE IF RND(1)>.84 T
HEN CO=CO-1
170 IF RND(1)>.84 AND RO=16 AND A(RO,8)=1
THEN PRINT:PRINT "You hear a whispered voi
ce warning you:":PRINT "'You must do somet
hing about the dwarf'"
180 PRINT:PRINT "Your attributes are:"
190 PRINT TAB(4);"Strength -"ST"  Charisma
 -"CH
200 PRINT TAB(4);"Dexterity -"DE"  Intelli
gence -"IT
210 PRINT TAB(4);"Wisdom -"WI"  Constituti
on -"CO
220 IF ST*CH*DE*IT*WI*CO=0 THEN PRINT "You
 are exhausted...":PRINT "so this adventur
e must end":QU=2:GOTO 2590
230 FLAG=0
240 FOR J=1 TO 5
250 IF P(J)<>0 THEN FLAG=1
260 NEXT J
270 IF FLAG=0 THEN 340
280 CASH=0
290 PRINT:PRINT "You are carrying:"
300 FOR J=1 TO 5
310 IF P(J)<>0 THEN PRINT TAB(4);O$(P(J)):
CASH=CASH+V(P(J))
320 NEXT J
330 IF CASH>0 THEN PRINT TAB(8);"Total val
ue - $";STR$(CASH)
340 PRINT
350 REM ***************
360 REM INPUT HANDLING
370 KW=0:REM =1 IF WORD UNDERSTOOD
380 FOR Z=1 TO 1000:NEXT Z
390 INPUT "What do you want to do";A$
400 IF A$="" THEN 390
410 AS=ASC(A$)
420 IF AS<65 OR AS>90 THEN PRINT TAB(3);">
>> CAPITAL LETTERS, PLEASE":PRINT:GOTO 390
```

```
430 M=LEN(A$):IF M<7 THEN A$=A$+" ":GOTO 4
30
440 B$=LEFT$(A$,3)
450 IF B$="HEL" THEN PRINT "NO HELP FOR MO
RTALS IN THIS GAME!":PRINT"...although rea
ding and drinking":PRINT "may help...":GOT
O 40
460 IF B$="QUI" THEN QU=4:GOTO 2530
470 N=1
480 IF MID$(A$,N,1)=" " THEN C$=MID$(A$,N+
1,3):IF LEFT$(C$,1)<>" " THEN 530 ELSE 500

490 IF N<M THEN N=N+1:GOTO 480
500 IF RND(1)>.5 THEN 520
510 PRINT TAB(6);"BY ITSELF,";A$:PRINT TAB
(6);"CAN'T BE ACTED ON":GOTO 390
520 PRINT A$;" IS JUST ONE WORD":PRINT TAB
(4);"I NEED TWO":GOTO 390
530 IF RO<>8 AND RO<>34 THEN 560
540 IF B$="STA" OR B$="KIL" OR B$="FIG" OR
 B$="KIC" OR B$="PUN" OR B$="SLA" OR B$="A
TT" THEN KW=1:GOSUB 1400
550 IF A(RO,7)>98 AND B$<>"UNL" THEN PRINT
 TAB(4);"** The doors are locked **":GOTO
40
560 IF B$="STA" OR B$="KIL" OR B$="FIG" OR
 B$="KIC" OR B$="PUN" OR B$="SLA" OR B$="A
TT" THEN KW=1:GOSUB 1400
570 IF B$="GO " OR B$="MOV" OR B$="CLI" OR
 B$="RUN" OR B$="WAL" THEN KW=1:GOSUB 740
580 IF B$="TAK" OR B$="GET" OR B$="STE" OR
 B$="LIF" THEN KW=1:GOSUB 950
590 IF B$="DRO" OR B$="PUT" OR B$="THR" OR
 B$="BRE" THEN KW=1:GOSUB 1160
600 IF B$="UNL" THEN KW=1:GOSUB 2360
610 IF B$="OPE" THEN KW=1:GOSUB 2660
620 IF B$="REA" THEN KW=1:GOSUB 2750
630 IF B$="DRI" OR B$="SWA" THEN KW=1:GOSU
B 2870
640 IF B$="BRI" OR B$="PAY" THEN KW=1:GOSU
B 3000
650 IF KW=1 THEN 700
660 R=INT(RND(1)*3)
670 IF R=0 THEN PRINT "IT WOULD NOT BE WIS
```

```
E TO ";A$
680 IF R=1 THEN PRINT "ONLY A FOOL WOULD T
RY TO ";A$
690 IF R=2 THEN PRINT "I DON'T UNDERSTAND
'";A$
700 FOR Z=1 TO 500:NEXT Z
710 GOTO 40
720 REM * END OF MAJOR HANDLING LOOP *
730 REM ********
740 REM MOVEMENT
750 IF RO<>16 OR A(16,8)<>1 THEN 800
760 PRINT:PRINT "The dwarf refuses to let"

770 PRINT TAB(9);"you proceed..."
780 FOR Z=1 TO 500:NEXT
790 RETURN
800 C$=LEFT$(C$,1)
810 IF C$="N" AND A(RO,1)=0 THEN PRINT "Yo
u cannot go that way":RETURN
820 IF C$="S" AND A(RO,2)=0 THEN PRINT "Th
ere is no exit south":RETURN
830 IF C$="E" AND A(RO,3)=0 THEN PRINT "I
see nowhere to the east to go":RETURN
840 IF C$="W" AND A(RO,4)=0 THEN PRINT "Ev
en you cannot walk through walls":RETURN
850 IF C$="U" AND A(RO,5)=0 THEN PRINT "Th
ere is no way to move up":RETURN
860 IF C$="D" AND A(RO,6)=0 THEN PRINT "Yo
u cannot descend from here":RETURN
870 IF C$="N" THEN RO=A(RO,1)
880 IF C$="S" THEN RO=A(RO,2)
890 IF C$="E" THEN RO=A(RO,3)
900 IF C$="W" THEN RO=A(RO,4)
910 IF C$="U" THEN RO=A(RO,5)
920 IF C$="D" THEN RO=A(RO,6)
930 RETURN
940 REM ******************
950 REM GET OBJECTS ROUTINE
960 FLAG=0
970 FOR J=1 TO 5
980 IF P(J)<>0 THEN FLAG=FLAG+1
990 NEXT J
1000 IF FLAG=5 THEN PRINT "You are already
 carrying your":PRINT "maximum of five obj
```

```
ects":RETURN
1010 IF C$="CHE" THEN PRINT "It is far too
 heavy to lift":RETURN
1020 IF A(RO,7)=0 AND A(RO,9)=0 AND A(RO,1
0)=0 THEN PRINT "I see nothing to pick up"
:RETURN
1030 D$="":E$="":F$="":N=0
1040 D$=LEFT$(O$(A(RO,7)),3)
1050 E$=LEFT$(O$(A(RO,9)),3)
1060 F$=LEFT$(O$(A(RO,10)),3)
1070 IF C$=D$ THEN N=A(RO,7):A(RO,7)=0
1080 IF C$=E$ THEN N=A(RO,9):A(RO,9)=0
1090 IF C$=F$ THEN N=A(RO,10):A(RO,10)=0
1100 J=1
1110 IF P(J)=0 THEN P(J)=N:GOTO 1130
1120 IF J<5 THEN J=J+1:GOTO 1110
1130 IF N>0 THEN PRINT TAB(3);">->YOU NOW
 HAVE THE ";O$(N)
1140 RETURN
1150 REM *************
1160 REM DROP ROUTINE
1170 FLAG=0
1180 FOR J=1 TO 5
1190 IF P(J)<>0 THEN FLAG=1
1200 NEXT J
1210 IF FLAG=0 THEN PRINT "You are not car
rying anything":RETURN
1220 IF A(RO,7)<>0 AND A(RO,9)<>0 AND A(RO
,10)<>0 THEN PRINT "This room already hold
s its":PRINT TAB(6);"maximum objects":RETU
RN
1230 D$="":D=0
1240 FOR J=1 TO 18
1250 IF LEFT$(O$(J),3)=C$ THEN D$=O$(J):D=
J
1260 NEXT J
1270 IF D$="" THEN PRINT TAB(3);"How can y
ou when you're":PRINT TAB(5);"not holding
it?":RETURN
1280 FOR J=1 TO 5
1290 IF P(J)=D THEN P(J)=0
1300 NEXT J
1310 IF A(RO,7)=0 THEN A(RO,7)=D:GOTO 1340
```

```
1320 IF A(RO,9)=0 THEN A(RO,9)=D:GOTO 1340

1330 IF A(RO,10)=0 THEN A(RO,10)=D
1340 IF B$="DRO" THEN PRINT "YOU HAVE DROP
PED THE ";D$
1350 IF B$="PUT" THEN PRINT "YOU HAVE PUT
THE ";D$;" DOWN"
1360 IF B$="THR" THEN PRINT "WITH A MIGHTY
 HEAVE, YOU":PRINT "THROW THE ";D$;" AWAY"

1370 IF B$="BRE" THEN PRINT "YOU HAVE BROK
EN THE ";D$
1380 RETURN
1390 REM **************
1400 REM FIGHT ROUTINE
1410 IF A(RO,8)=1 THEN PRINT "The dwarf re
fuses to fight":PRINT "and his magic prote
cts him":RETURN
1420 IF A(RO,8)<>0 THEN 1470
1430 R=RND(1)
1440 IF R<.5 THEN PRINT "There is nothing
to fight here"
1450 IF R>=.5 THEN PRINT "You can't fight
empty air!"
1460 RETURN
1470 G$=M$(A(RO,8))
1480 S1=INT(RND(1)*6+RND(1)*6+RND(1)*6)+3
1490 H1=INT(RND(1)*6+RND(1)*6+RND(1)*6)+3
1500 D1=INT(RND(1)*6+RND(1)*6+RND(1)*6)+3
1510 I1=INT(RND(1)*6+RND(1)*6+RND(1)*6)+3
1520 W1=INT(RND(1)*6+RND(1)*6+RND(1)*6)+3
1530 C1=INT(RND(1)*6+RND(1)*6+RND(1)*6)+3
1540 PRINT "-------------------------------
---------"
1550 PRINT "YOUR OPPONENT IS A ";G$
1560 MT=0:HT=0:REM MONSTER TALLY, HUMAN TA
LLY
1570 FF=S1*(INT(RND(1)*6)+1)
1580 PRINT:PRINT "-------------------------
---------------"
1590 PRINT "THE ";G$;"'S DANGER LEVEL IS"F
F
1600 FOR Z=1 TO 1500:NEXT Z
1610 FOR J=1 TO 5
```

```
1620 T(J)=0
1630 IF P(J)=1 THEN PRINT "YOUR AXE COULD
BE HANDY":T(J)=1
1640 IF P(J)=2 THEN PRINT "YOUR SKILL WITH
 THE SWORD":PRINT "MAY STAND YOU IN GOOD S
TEAD":T(J)=2
1650 IF P(J)=3 THEN PRINT "YOUR DAGGER IS
USEFUL AGAINST ";G$;"S":T(J)=3
1660 IF P(J)=4 THEN PRINT "THE MACE WILL M
AKE SHORT WORK OF IT":T(J)=4
1670 IF P(J)=5 THEN PRINT "YOUR QUARTERSTA
FF WILL GIVE":PRINT "IT NO QUARTER...":T(J
)=5
1680 IF P(J)=6 THEN PRINT "SWINGING YOUR M
ORNING STAR MAY INFLICT":PRINT "HEAVY WOUN
DS ON THE ";G$:T(J)=6
1690 IF P(J)=7 THEN PRINT "A FALCHION IS A
 USEFUL WEAPON":T(J)=7
1700 NEXT J
1710 FLAG=0
1720 FOR J=1 TO 5
1730 IF T(J)<>0 THEN FLAG=FLAG+1
1740 NEXT J
1750 IF FLAG=0 THEN PRINT "YOU MUST FIGHT
THE ";G$;" WITH":PRINT "YOUR BARE HANDS":G
OTO 1910
1760 IF FLAG>1 THEN 1830
1770 FOR J=1 TO 5
1780 IF T(J)<>0 THEN FLAG=T(J)
1790 NEXT J
1800 PRINT "YOU MUST FIGHT WITH YOUR ";O$(
FLAG)
1810 FF=INT(FF*2/FLAG)
1820 GOTO 1910
1830 PRINT "CHOOSE YOUR WEAPON:"
1840 FOR J=1 TO 5
1850 IF P(J)<>0 THEN PRINT J;" - ";O$(J)
1860 NEXT J
1870 INPUT "Enter the number to choose";J
1880 IF P(J)=0 THEN PRINT "YOU DO NOT HAVE
 THE ";O$(J):GOTO 1870
1890 PRINT "RIGHT, SO YOU CHOOSE TO FIGHT"
:PRINT "WITH THE ";O$(J)
1900 FF=INT(FF*2/J)
```

```
1910 FOR Z=1 TO 1500:NEXT Z
1920 PRINT "THE ";G$;" HAS THE FOLLOWING A
TTRIBUTES:"
1930 PRINT "1 - Strength"S1"  2 - Charisma
";H1
1940 PRINT "3 - Dexterity"D1" 4 - Intellig
ence"I1
1950 PRINT "5 - Wisdom"W1"    6 - Constitu
tion"C1
1960 PRINT:PRINT "YOUR ATTRIBUTES ARE:"
1970 PRINT "1 - Strength"ST"  2 - Charisma
"CH
1980 PRINT "3 - Dexterity"DE" 4 - Intellig
ence"IT
1990 PRINT "5 - Wisdom"WI"    6 - Constitu
tion"CO
2000 PRINT:PRINT "Which attributes will yo
u fight":PRINT "with (2)";
2010 INPUT Z,Q
2020 IF Z<1 OR Q<1 OR Z>6 OR Q>6 OR Z=Q TH
EN PRINT "DO NOT FOOL AROUND WHEN A ";G$:P
RINT "IS IN THE ROOM WITH YOU!":GOTO 2010
2030 IF Z=1 OR Q=1 THEN MT=MT+S1:HT=HT+ST
2040 IF Z=2 OR Q=2 THEN MT=MT+H1:HT=HT+CH
2050 IF Z=3 OR Q=3 THEN MT=MT+D1:HT=HT+DE
2060 IF Z=4 OR Q=4 THEN MT=MT+I1:HT=HT+IT
2070 IF Z=5 OR Q=5 THEN MT=MT+W1:HT=HT+WI
2080 IF Z=6 OR Q=6 THEN MT=MT+C1:HT=HT+CO
2090 IF HT=MT THEN PRINT TAB(10);"You are
evenly matched":GOTO 2130
2100 PRINT "IT LOOKS LIKE THE ODDS"
2110 PRINT "ARE IN FAVOR OF ";
2120 IF HT>MT THEN PRINT "YOU" ELSE PRINT
"THE ";G$
2130 K=INT(RND(1)*7)
2140 FOR Z=1 TO 700:NEXT Z
2150 PRINT "THE ";G$;" -"MT
2160 PRINT "YOU -"HT:PRINT
2170 IF K=0 THEN PRINT "You struck a splen
did blow!":MT=MT-1
2180 IF K=1 THEN PRINT "THE ";G$;" STRIKES
 OUT":HT=HT-3:ST=ST-1:CH=CH-1
2190 IF K=2 THEN PRINT "YOU DRAW THE ";G$;
"'S BLOOD":MT=MT-1
```

```
2200 IF K=3 THEN PRINT "You are wounded!!"
:HT=HT-INT(RND(1)*3)-1:DE=DE-1
2210 IF K=4 THEN PRINT "THE ";G$;" IS TIRI
NG":MT=MT-1
2220 IF K=5 THEN PRINT "You are bleeding..
.":HT=HT-2:WI=WI-1:CO=CO-1
2230 IF K=6 THEN PRINT "YOU WOUND THE ";G$
:MT=MT-1
2240 IF RND(1)>.25 AND HT>0 AND MT>0 THEN
FOR T=1 TO 1600:NEXT T:GOTO 2130
2250 IF HT>MT THEN PRINT "YOU HAVE SLAIN T
HE ";G$:MK=MK+1:GOTO 2330
2260 PRINT "THE ";G$;" GOT THE BETTER OF":
PRINT "YOU THAT TIME..."
2270 IF Z=1 OR Q=1 THEN ST=4*INT(ST/5)
2280 IF Z=2 OR Q=2 THEN CH=3*INT(CH/4)
2290 IF Z=3 OR Q=3 THEN DE=6*INT(DE/7)
2300 IF Z=4 OR Q=4 THEN IT=2*INT(IT/3)
2310 IF Z=5 OR Q=5 THEN WI=5*INT(WI/6)
2320 IF Z=6 OR Q=6 THEN CO=INT(CO/2)
2330 A(RO,8)=0
2340 RETURN
2350 REM *************
2360 REM UNLOCK DOORS
2370 IF RO<>8 AND RO<>34 OR A(RO,7)<99 THE
N PRINT "There is no locked door in this r
oom":RETURN
2380 FLAG=0
2390 T=0
2400 FOR J=1 TO 5
2410 IF P(J)=17 THEN FLAG=1:T=J
2420 IF P(J)=18 THEN FLAG=2:T=J
2430 NEXT J
2440 IF FLAG=0 THEN PRINT "You do not have
 a key!":RETURN
2450 IF FLAG=2 AND RO=8 OR FLAG=1 AND RO=3
4 THEN PRINT "That key does not fit this d
oor":RETURN
2460 PRINT "There is a creak as the key tu
rns"
2470 FOR Z=1 TO 1300:NEXT Z
2480 PRINT ".....THE DOOR IS NOW UNLOCKED.
.."
2490 A(RO,7)=0
```

```
2500 P(T)=0
2510 RETURN
2520 REM ***********
2530 REM END OF GAME
2540 SC=0:REM SCORE
2550 IF QU=4 THEN PRINT "I did not imagine
 you would turn":PRINT TAB(5);"out to be a
 quitter!":GOTO 2590
2560 PRINT:PRINT "CONGRATULATIONS! You hav
e completed":PRINT TAB(7);"THE ADVENTURE"
2570 SC=100
2580 PRINT:PRINT
2590 SC=(SC+20*CASH+47*MK+ST+2*CH+3*DE+4+I
T+5*WI+6*CO)/QU
2600 IF MK>0 THEN PRINT "YOU KILLED"MK"MON
STERS"
2610 IF MK>0 AND CASH>0 THEN PRINT "AND ";

2620 PRINT:PRINT "YOU FOUND $";STR$(CASH);
" WORTH":PRINT TAB(8);"OF TREASURE"
2630 PRINT:PRINT "Your score for this Adve
nture is"SC
2640 END
2650 REM **********
2660 REM OPEN CHEST
2670 FLAG=0
2680 IF C$<>"CHE" THEN PRINT "THAT WOULD N
OT BE WISE":RETURN
2690 IF RO<>13 AND RO<>40 THEN PRINT "I CA
NNOT SEE ANYTHING TO OPEN HERE":RETURN
2700 IF BOX=1 THEN IF RND(1)>.6 THEN PRINT
 TAB(4);"It holds nothing but dust...":RET
URN
2710 IF RO=13 OR BOX=1 THEN PRINT "IT IS E
MPTY!":RETURN
2720 IF BOX=0 THEN PRINT "INSIDE YOU FIND
A PARCHMENT, WITH":PRINT "THE FOLLOWING ME
SSAGE: 'A little":PRINT "man can be bound
by gold'":BOX=1
2730 RETURN
2740 REM ***********
2750 REM READ SCROLL
2760 FLAG=0
2770 FOR J=1 TO 5
```

```
2780 IF P(J)=12 THEN FLAG=1
2790 NEXT J
2800 IF FLAG=0 THEN PRINT "You are not hol
ding anything":PRINT "which you can read":
RETURN
2810 R=INT(RND(1)*3)
2820 IF R=0 THEN PRINT "It says 'THE LOCKS
 NEED SPECIAL KEYS'"
2830 IF R=1 THEN PRINT "The scroll reads:'
CHESTS CAN CONTAIN AID'"
2840 IF R=2 THEN PRINT "It says 'THE AMULE
T IS IMPORTANT'"
2850 RETURN
2860 REM *************
2870 REM DRINK POTION
2880 FLAG=0
2890 FOR J=1 TO 5
2900 IF P(J)=13 THEN FLAG=J
2910 NEXT J
2920 IF FLAG=0 THEN PRINT "YOU CAN'T DRINK
 ";C$:RETURN
2930 PRINT "You are instantly filled with"
:PRINT "healing, and your strength is rest
ored"
2940 PRINT "The bottle holding the potion"

2950 PRINT "magically fades from view..."
2960 ST=20
2970 P(FLAG)=0
2980 RETURN
2990 REM ************
3000 REM BRIBE DWARF
3010 IF A(RO,8)<>1 THEN PRINT "YOU SHOULDN
'T TRY THAT":PRINT "WITH A ";M$(A(RO,8)):R
ETURN
3020 PRINT "He demands the amulet!"
3030 FLAG=0
3040 FOR J=1 TO 5
3050 IF P(J)=9 THEN FLAG=J
3060 NEXT J
3070 IF FLAG<>0 THEN 3250
3080 PRINT "YOU DO NOT HAVE IT..."
3090 FOR T=1 TO 1000:NEXT T
3100 IF RND(1)>.5 THEN PRINT "HE WOULD ACC
```

```
EPT ANYTHING":PRINT "THAT HE REALLY WANTS"
:GOTO 3210
3110 PRINT "HE DECIDES, HOWEVER, TO ACCEPT
"
3120 PRINT "A 'GIFT' OF ";
3130 FOR J=1 TO 5
3140 IF P(J)<>0 THEN FLAG=J
3150 NEXT J
3160 IF FLAG=0 THEN 3200
3170 PRINT "THE ";O$(FLAG)
3180 P(FLAG)=0
3190 GOTO 3270
3200 PRINT "ANYTHING VALUABLE"
3210 PRINT:PRINT "BUT YOU HAVE NOTHING"
3220 PRINT "AND SO HE KILLS YOU!!"
3230 QU=3
3240 GOTO 2570
3250 PRINT "Lucky for you that you had it!
"
3260 P(FLAG)=0
3270 A(RO,8)=0
3280 RETURN
3290 REM ******************
3300 REM ROOM DESCRIPTIONS
3310 IF RO>11 THEN 4140
3320 ON RO GOSUB 3340,3380,3450,3530,3620,
3720,3790,3840,3920,3990,4060
3330 RETURN
3340 REM ROOM ONE
3350 PRINT "You are out on the battlements
 of the"
3360 PRINT "chateau. There is only one way
 back"
3370 RETURN
3380 REM ROOM TWO
3390 PRINT "This is an eerie room, where o
nce"
3400 PRINT "magicians convorted with evil"

3410 PRINT "sprites and werebeasts..."
3420 PRINT "Exits lead in three directions
"
3430 PRINT "An evil smell comes from the s
outh"
```

```
3440 RETURN
3450 REM ROOM THREE
3460 PRINT "An old straw mattress lies in
one"
3470 PRINT "corner...it has been ripped ap
art to"
3480 PRINT "find any treasure which was hi
dden in it"
3490 PRINT "Light comes fitfully from a wi
ndow to"
3500 PRINT "the north, and around the door
s to"
3510 PRINT "south, east and west"
3520 RETURN
3530 REM ROOM FOUR
3540 PRINT "This wooden-panelled room make
s"
3550 PRINT "you feel damp and uncomfortabl
e"
3560 IF RND(1)>.5 THEN PRINT "A mouse scam
pers across the floor" ELSE PRINT "A bat f
lits across the ceiling"
3570 PRINT "There are three doors leading"

3580 PRINT "from this room, one made of ir
on"
3590 PRINT "Your sixth sense warns you to"

3600 PRINT "choose carefully..."
3610 RETURN
3620 REM ROOM FIVE
3630 PRINT "You ignore your intuition..."
3640 PRINT "A Spell of Living Stone, prime
d"
3650 PRINT "to trap the first intruder has
"
3660 PRINT "been set on you...with your la
st"
3670 PRINT "seconds of life you have time"

3680 PRINT "only to feel profound regret..
."
3690 QU=2
3700 SC=50
```

```
3710 GOTO 2590
3720 REM ROOM SIX
3730 PRINT "You are in an L-shaped room"
3740 PRINT "Heavy parchment lines the wall
s"
3750 PRINT "You can see through an archway
"
3760 PRINT "to the east...but that is not"

3770 PRINT "the only exit from this room"
3780 RETURN
3790 REM ROOM SEVEN
3800 PRINT "There is an archway to the wes
t,"
3810 PRINT "leading to an L-shaped room"
3820 PRINT "a door leads in the opposite d
irection"
3830 RETURN
3840 REM ROOM EIGHT
3850 PRINT "This must be the Chateau's mai
n kitchen"
3860 PRINT "but any food left here has lon
g"
3870 PRINT "rotted away..."
3880 PRINT
3890 PRINT "A door leads to the north, and
"
3900 PRINT "there is one to the west"
3910 RETURN
3920 REM ROOM NINE
3930 PRINT "You find yourself in a small,"

3940 PRINT "room...which makes you feel"
3950 PRINT "claustrophobic...":PRINT
3960 PRINT "There is a picture of a black"

3970 PRINT "dragon painted on the north"
3980 PRINT "wall, above the door..."
3990 REM ROOM TEN
4000 PRINT "A stairwell ends in this room,
 which"
4010 PRINT "more of a landing than a real"
4020 PRINT "room. The door to the north is
"
```

```
4030 PRINT "made of iron, which has rusted
"
4040 PRINT "over the centuries..."
4050 RETURN
4060 REM ROOM ELEVEN
4070 PRINT "There is a stone archway to th
e north,"
4080 PRINT "You are in a very long room."
4090 PRINT:PRINT "Fresh air blows down som
e stairs"
4100 PRINT "and rich red drapes cover
4110 PRINT "the walls...You can see doors"

4120 PRINT "to the south and east"
4130 RETURN
4140 IF RO>22 THEN 5030
4150 ON RO-11 GOSUB 4170,4240,4330,4390,44
60,4530,4610,4710,4760,4890,4970
4160 RETURN
4170 REM ROOM TWELVE
4180 PRINT "You have entered a room filled
"
4190 PRINT "with swirling, choking smoke."
:PRINT
4200 PRINT "You must leave quickly to rema
in"
4210 PRINT "healthy enough to continue"
4220 PRINT "your chosen quest..."
4230 RETURN
4240 REM ROOM THIRTEEN
4250 PRINT "There is a mirror in the corne
r"
4260 PRINT "You glance at it, and feel"
4270 PRINT "suddenly very ill.":PRINT
4280 PRINT "You realise the looking-glass
has"
4290 PRINT "been enfused with a Spell of C
harisma"
4300 PRINT "Reduction...oh dear..."
4310 CH=CH-1
4320 RETURN
4330 REM ROOM FOURTEEN
4340 PRINT "This room is richly finished,
with"
```

```
4350 PRINT "a white marble floor. Strange"

4360 PRINT "footprints lead to the two doo
rs"
4370 PRINT "from this room...Dare you foll
ow them?"
4380 RETURN
4390 REM ROOM FIFTEEN
4400 PRINT "You are in a long, long"
4410 PRINT "hallway, lined on each side"
4420 PRINT "with rich, red drapes..."
4430 PRINT:PRINT "They are parted halfway
down"
4440 PRINT "the east wall where there is a
 door"
4450 RETURN
4460 REM ROOM SIXTEEN
4470 PRINT "Someone has spent a long time"

4480 PRINT "painting this room a bright ye
llow..."
4490 PRINT:PRINT "You remember reading tha
t"
4500 PRINT "yellow is the Ancient Oracle's
"
4510 PRINT "Color of Warning..."
4520 RETURN
4530 REM ROOM SEVENTEEN - START
4540 PRINT "As you stumble down the ladder
"
4550 PRINT "you fall into the room. The la
dder"
4560 PRINT "crashes down behind you...ther
e"
4570 PRINT "is now no way back..."
4580 PRINT:PRINT "A small door leads east
from"
4590 PRINT "this very cramped room..."
4600 RETURN
4610 REM ROOM EIGHTEEN
4620 PRINT "You find yourself in a Hall of
"
4630 PRINT "Mirrors...and see yourself"
4640 PRINT "reflected a hundred times or"
```

```
4650 PRINT "more...Through the bright glar
e"
4660 PRINT "you can make out doors in all"

4670 PRINT "directions...You notice the"
4680 PRINT "mirrors around the east door"
4690 PRINT "are heavily tarnished..."
4700 RETURN
4710 REM ROOM NINETEEN
4720 PRINT "You find yourself in a long co
rridor..."
4730 FOR Z=1 TO 1000:NEXT Z
4740 PRINT "Your footsteps echo as you wal
k"
4750 RETURN
4760 REM ROOM TWENTY
4770 PRINT "You feel as you've been wander
ing"
4780 PRINT "around this chateau for ever..
."
4790 PRINT "and you begin to despair of ev
er"
4800 PRINT "escaping..."
4810 PRINT:PRINT "Still, you can't get too
 depressed, but"
4820 PRINT "must struggle on. Looking arou
nd, you"
4830 PRINT "see you are in a room which ha
s a"
4840 PRINT "heavy timbered ceiling, and wh
ite"
4850 PRINT "roughly-finished walls..."
4860 PRINT:PRINT "There are two doors..."
4870 FOR Z=1 TO 1000:NEXT Z
4880 RETURN
4890 REM ROOM TWENTY-ONE
4900 PRINT "You are in a small alcove. You
"
4910 PRINT "look around...but can see noth
ing in"
4920 PRINT "gloom...perhaps if you wait a"

4930 PRINT "while your eyes will adjust to
 the"
```

```
4940 PRINT "murky dark of this alcove..."
4950 FOR Z=1 TO 2000:NEXT:RETURN
4960 RETURN
4970 REM ROOM TWENTY-TWO
4980 PRINT "A dried-up fountain stands in
the"
4990 PRINT "center of this courtyard, whic
h"
5000 PRINT "once held beautiful flowers...
but"
5010 PRINT "have long since died..."
5020 RETURN
5030 IF RO>33 THEN 5890
5040 ON RO-22 GOSUB 5060,5110,5160,5230,52
80,5380,5450,5530,5590,5680,5840
5050 RETURN
5060 REM ROOM TWENTY-THREE
5070 PRINT "The scent of dying flowers fil
ls"
5080 PRINT "this brightly-lit room..."
5090 PRINT:PRINT "There are two exits from
 it.."
5100 RETURN
5110 REM ROOM TWENTY-FOUR
5120 PRINT "This is a round stone cavern"
5130 PRINT "off the side of the alcove to"

5140 PRINT "your north..."
5150 RETURN
5160 REM ROOM TWENTY-FIVE
5170 PRINT "You are in an enormous circula
r"
5180 PRINT "room, which looks as if it was
"
5190 PRINT "used as a games room. Rubble c
overs"
5200 PRINT "the floor, partially blocking"

5210 PRINT "the only exit..."
5220 RETURN
5230 REM ROOM TWENTY-SIX
5240 PRINT "Through the dim mustiness of"
5250 PRINT "this small potting shed you ca
n"
```

```
5260 PRINT "see a stairwell..."
5270 RETURN
5280 REM ROOM TWENTY-SEVEN - START
5290 PRINT "You begin this Adventure in a
small"
5300 PRINT "wood outside the Chateau..."
5310 FOR Z=1 TO 3000:NEXT Z
5320 PRINT:PRINT "While out walking one da
y, you come"
5330 PRINT "across a small, ramshackle she
d in"
5340 PRINT "the woods. Entering it, you se
e a"
5350 PRINT "hole in one corner...an old la
dder"
5360 PRINT "leads down from the hole..."
5370 RETURN
5380 REM ROOM TWENTY-EIGHT - END
5390 PRINT "How wonderful! Fresh air, sunl
ight..."
5400 FOR Z=1 TO 1000:NEXT Z
5410 PRINT:PRINT "Birds are singing...you"

5420 PRINT "are free at last...."
5430 PRINT:PRINT
5440 GOTO 2560
5450 REM ROOM TWENTY NINE
5460 PRINT "The smell came from bodies"
5470 PRINT "rotting in huge traps..."
5480 FOR Z=1 TO 1000:NEXT Z
5490 PRINT "One springs shut on you,"
5500 PRINT "trapping you forever"
5510 QU=3.5
5520 GOTO 2570
5530 REM ROOM THIRTY
5540 PRINT "You fall into a pit of flames.
.."
5550 IF RND(1)>.7 THEN 5540
5560 SC=10
5570 QU=3.4
5580 GOTO 2590
5590 REM ROOM THIRTY-ONE
5600 PRINT "Aaaaahhh...you have fallen int
o"
```

```
5610 FOR Z=1 TO 3000:NEXT Z
5620 PRINT "a pool of acid...now you know
- too"
5630 PRINT "late - why the mirrors were"
5640 PRINT "so badly tarnished"
5650 SC=20
5660 QU=3
5670 GOTO 2590
5680 REM ROOM THIRTY-TWO
5690 PRINT "It's too bad you chose that ex
it"
5700 PRINT "from the alcove..."
5710 FOR Z=1 TO 2000:NEXT Z
5720 PRINT "A giant Funnel-Web Spider leap
s"
5730 PRINT "on you...and before you can re
act"
5740 PRINT "bites you on the neck...you"
5750 PRINT "have 10 seconds to live..."
5760 FOR T= 10 TO 1 STEP -1
5770 PRINT TAB(T);T
5780 FOR Z=1 TO 300:NEXT Z
5790 PRINT
5800 NEXT T
5810 SC=3
5820 QU=5
5830 GOTO 2590
5840 REM ROOM THIRTY-THREE
5850 PRINT "A stairwell leads into this ro
om, a"
5860 PRINT "poor and common hovel with man
y"
5870 PRINT "doors and exits..."
5880 RETURN
5890 ON RO-33 GOSUB 5920,5970,6030,6100,62
40,6310,6360,6430,6510,6560,6600
5900 RETURN
5910 REM **DESCRIPTIONS**
5920 REM ROOM THIRTY-FOUR
5930 PRINT "It is hard to see in this room
,"
5940 PRINT "and you slip slightly on the"
5950 PRINT "uneven, rocky floor..."
5960 RETURN
```

```
5970 REM ROOM THIRTY-FIVE
5980 PRINT "Horrors! This room was once"
5990 PRINT "the torture chamber of the Cha
teau.."
6000 PRINT:PRINT "Skeletons lie on the flo
or, still"
6010 PRINT "with chains around the bones..
."
6020 RETURN
6030 REM ROOM THIRTY-SIX
6040 PRINT "Another room with very unpleas
ant"
6050 PRINT "memories..."
6060 FOR Z=1 TO 1000:NEXT Z
6070 PRINT:PRINT "This foul hole was used
as the"
6080 PRINT "Chateau dungeon...."
6090 RETURN
6100 REM ROOM THIRTY-SEVEN
6110 PRINT "Oh no, this is a Gargoyle's la
ir..."
6120 FOR Z=1 TO 1000:NEXT Z
6130 PRINT "It has been held prisoner here
 for"
6140 PRINT "three hundred years..."
6150 FOR Z=1 TO 1000:NEXT Z
6160 PRINT:PRINT "In his frenzy he thrashe
s out at you..."
6170 FOR Z=1 TO 1000:NEXT Z
6180 PRINT TAB(12);"and..."
6190 FOR Z=1 TO 1000:NEXT Z
6200 PRINT "...breaks your neck!!"
6210 SC=0
6220 QU=3
6230 GOTO 2590
6240 REM ROOM THIRTY-EIGHT
6250 PRINT "This was the Lower Dancing Hal
l..."
6260 PRINT "With doors to the north, the e
ast"
6270 PRINT "and to the west, you would see
m to be"
6280 PRINT "able to flee any danger..."
6290 FOR Z=1 TO 1000:NEXT Z
```

```
6300 RETURN
6310 REM ROOM THIRTY-NINE
6320 PRINT "This is a dingy pit at the foo
t of"
6330 PRINT "some extremely dubious-looking
"
6340 PRINT "stairs. A door leads to the ea
st..."
6350 RETURN
6360 REM ROOM FORTY
6370 PRINT "Doors open to each compass poi
nt from"
6380 PRINT "the Trophy Room of the Chateau
..."
6390 PRINT:PRINT "The heads of strange cre
atures shot"
6400 PRINT "by the ancestral owners are mo
unted"
6410 PRINT "high up on each wall..."
6420 RETURN
6430 REM ROOM FORTY-ONE
6440 PRINT "You have stumbled on a secret
room..."
6450 FOR Z=1 TO 1300:NEXT Z
6460 PRINT:PRINT "Down here, eons ago, the
 ancient"
6470 PRINT "Necromancers of Thorin plied t
heir"
6480 PRINT "evil craft...and the remnant o
f"
6490 PRINT "their spells hangs heavy on th
e air..."
6500 RETURN
6510 REM ROOM FORTY-TWO
6520 PRINT "Cobwebs brush your face as you
 make"
6530 PRINT "your way through the gloom of
this"
6540 PRINT "room of shadows..."
6550 RETURN
6560 REM ROOM FORTY-THREE
6570 PRINT "This gloomy passage lies at th
e"
```

```
6580 PRINT "intersection of three rooms..."
6590 RETURN
6600 REM ROOM FORTY-FOUR
6610 PRINT "You are in the rear turret roo
m, below"
6620 PRINT "the extreme western wall of th
e"
6630 PRINT "ancient chateau..."
6640 RETURN
6650 REM *****************
6660 REM DESCRIBE OBJECTS
6670 PRINT
6680 IF A(RO,7)>98 AND A(RO,9)=0 AND A(RO,
10)=0 THEN RETURN
6690 PRINT TAB(3)"YOU CAN SEE ";
6700 IF A(RO,7)>98 THEN 6720
6710 IF A(RO,7)<>0 THEN PRINT O$(A(RO,7))
6720 IF A(RO,9)>98 THEN 6740
6730 IF A(RO,9)<>0 THEN PRINT O$(A(RO,9))
6740 IF A(RO,10)>98 THEN 6760
6750 IF A(RO,10)<>0 THEN PRINT O$(A(RO,10)
)
6760 FOR Z=1 TO 500:NEXT Z
6770 PRINT
6780 RETURN
6790 REM **********
6800 REM INITIALISE
6810 CLS
6820 IF INKEY$<>"" THEN 6820
6830 N=0
6840 PRINT "PRESS ANY KEY TO START THE ADV
ENTURE"
6850 IF INKEY$="" THEN N=N+1:GOTO 6850
6860 RANDOMIZE N
6870 CLS
6880 PRINT:PRINT "Please stand by..."
6900 DIM A(44,10),P(5),O$(20),V(20),M$(20)
,T(5)
6910 ST=INT(RND(1)*6+RND(1)*6+RND(1)*6)+3
6920 CH=INT(RND(1)*6+RND(1)*6+RND(1)*6)+3
6930 DE=INT(RND(1)*6+RND(1)*6+RND(1)*6)+3
6940 IT=INT(RND(1)*6+RND(1)*6+RND(1)*6)+3
6950 WI=INT(RND(1)*6+RND(1)*6+RND(1)*6)+3
```

```
6960 CO=INT(RND(1)*6+RND(1)*6+RND(1)*6)+3
6970 CASH=0:REM TREASURE
6980 RO=27:REM STARTING ROOM
6990 QU=1:REM END OF GAME FLAG
7000 MK=0:REM MONSTERS KILLED
7010 BOX=0:REM CHEST FLAG
7020 A(8,7)=99:REM LOCKED DOOR i
7030 A(34,7)=100:REM LOCKED DOOR ii
7040 A(40,7)=20:REM CHEST
7050 A(13,7)=19:REM CHEST
7060 A(16,8)=1:REM DWARF
7070 REM SET UP ROOMS
7080 FOR X=1 TO 44
7090 FOR Y=1 TO 10
7100 READ A(X,Y)
7110 NEXT Y
7120 NEXT X
7130 REM DISTRIBUTE TREASURE
7140 RESTORE 7830
7150 FOR Z=1 TO 20
7160 READ O$(Z), V(Z)
7170 NEXT Z
7180 FOR Q=1 TO 16
7190 Z=INT(RND(1)*44)+1
7200 IF Z=5 OR Z=17 OR Z=27 OR Z=29 OR Z=3
0 OR Z=31 OR Z=32 OR Z=37 THEN 7190
7210 IF A(Z,7)<>0 THEN 7190
7220 A(Z,7)=Q
7230 NEXT Q
7240 PRINT
7250 PRINT TAB(3);"Just a few moments more
..."
7260 REM DISTRIBUTE MONSTERS
7270 RESTORE 7870
7280 FOR J=1 TO 20
7290 READ M$(J)
7300 IF J=1 THEN 7350
7310 Z=INT(RND(1)*44)+1
7320 IF Z=5 OR Z=16 OR Z=17 OR Z=27 OR Z=2
9 OR Z=30 OR Z=31 OR Z=32 OR Z=37 THEN 731
0
7330 IF A(Z,8)<>0 THEN 7310
7340 A(Z,8)=J
7350 NEXT J
```

```
7360 RETURN
7370 REM ROOM DATA
7380 DATA 1,1,2,1,1,1,0,0,0,0:REM 1
7390 DATA 0,29,3,1,0,0,17,0,0,0:REM 2
7400 DATA 0,8,4,2,0,0,0,0,0:REM 3
7410 DATA 0,9,5,3,0,0,0,0,0:REM 4
7420 DATA 5,5,5,5,5,0,0,0,0:REM 5
7430 DATA 0,11,7,30,0,0,0,0,0:REM 6
7440 DATA 0,0,8,6,0,0,0,0,0:REM 7
7450 DATA 3,0,0,7,0,0,99,0,0,0:REM 8
7460 DATA 4,10,0,0,0,0,0,0,0:REM 9
7470 DATA 9,0,0,0,0,39,0,0,0,0:REM 10
7480 DATA 6,0,0,0,28,0,0,0,0,0:REM 11
7490 DATA 0,16,13,0,0,0,0,0,0:REM 12
7500 DATA 0,0,14,12,0,0,19,0,0,0:REM 13
7510 DATA 0,18,0,13,0,0,0,0,0:REM 14
7520 DATA 0,21,16,0,0,0,0,0,0:REM 15
7530 DATA 12,20,19,15,0,0,0,1,0,0:REM 16
7540 DATA 0,0,18,0,27,0,0,0,0,0:REM 17
7550 DATA 14,19,31,17,0,0,0,0,0:REM 18
7560 DATA 18,23,0,16,0,0,0,0,0:REM 19
7570 DATA 16,25,0,0,0,0,0,0,0:REM 20
7580 DATA 15,24,0,32,0,0,0,0,0:REM 21
7590 DATA 0,26,23,0,0,0,0,0,0:REM 22
7600 DATA 19,0,0,22,0,0,0,0,0:REM 23
7610 DATA 21,0,0,0,0,0,0,0,0:REM 24
7620 DATA 20,25,25,25,25,25,0,0,0,0:REM 25

7630 DATA 22,0,0,0,0,33,0,0,0,0:REM 26
7640 DATA 0,0,0,0,0,17,0,0,0,0:REM 27
7650 DATA 0,0,0,0,0,11,0,0,0,0:REM 28
7660 DATA 29,29,29,29,29,29,0,0,0,0:REM 29

7670 DATA 30,30,30,30,30,30,0,0,0,0:REM 30

7680 DATA 31,31,31,31,31,31,0,0,0,0:REM 31

7690 DATA 32,32,32,32,32,32,0,0,0,0:REM 32

7700 DATA 43,42,40,0,26,0,0,0,0,0:REM 33
7710 DATA 0,38,35,0,0,0,100,0,0,0:REM 34
7720 DATA 0,43,36,34,0,0,0,0,0,0:REM 35
7730 DATA 0,40,37,35,0,0,0,0,0,0:REM 36
7740 DATA 37,37,37,37,37,37,0,0,0,0:REM 37
```

```
7750 DATA 34,0,43,39,0,0,0,0,0,0:REM 38
7760 DATA 0,0,38,0,10,0,0,0,0,0:REM 39
7770 DATA 36,41,44,33,0,0,20,0,0,0:REM 40
7780 DATA 40,41,41,42,41,41,0,0,0,0:REM 41

7790 DATA 33,42,41,42,42,42,0,0,0,0:REM 42

7800 DATA 35,33,0,38,0,0,0,0,0,0:REM 43
7810 DATA 0,0,0,40,0,0,18,0,0,0:REM 44
7820 REM OBJECT/VALUE DATA
7830 DATA "AXE",0,"SWORD",0,"DAGGER",0,"MA
CE",0
7840 DATA "QUARTERSTAFF",0,"MORNING STAR",
0,"FALCHION",0
7850 DATA "CRYSTAL BALL",99,"AMULET",247,"
EBONY RING",166,"GEMS",462,"MYSTIC SCROLL"
,195,"HEALING POTION",231,"DILITHIUM CRYST
ALS",162,"COPPER PIECES",27,"DIADEM",141,"
SILVER KEY",0,"GOLDEN KEY",0,"CHEST OF STO
NE",0,"CHEST MADE OF IRON",0
7860 REM DATA MONSTERS
7870 DATA "DWARF","MONOCEROS","PARADRUS","
VAMPYRE","WRNACH","GIOLLA DACKER","KRAKEN"
,"FENRIS WOLF","CALOPUS","BASILISK"
7880 DATA "GRIMOIRE","FLYING BUFFALO","BER
SERKOID","WYRM","CROWTHERWOOD","GYGAX","RA
GNAROK","FOMORINE","HAFGYGR","GRENDEL"
```

23

ADDING EXCITEMENT

Finally, we'll look at a few ways you can add interest and "playability" to your programs.

The two most obvious things you should strive for are (a) unpredictability and (b) stability. These may seem to be mutually incompatible, but of course they are not. The unpredictability refers to the unknowns which a player must cope with when traversing the rocky plains of your Adventure. The stability refers to the environment which must (unless you have explicitly arranged for something different, such as a magician who causes the walls to shift every time you turn your head) be sufficiently stable and coherent to allow it to be mapped.

Map-Making

People who try to solve the Adventures you create enjoy making maps as they explore. To allow them to create maps, your Adventures should be relatively stable and coherent. As you've probably gathered, creating an initial map and a Travel Table from it, lies at the heart of Adventure programming. All else is commentary.

Get the map (and the Table) right and the rest should fall into place.

Structured Programming

As in all fields of human activity, conventions have developed in computer programming regarding a "better way" to do things. One of these ways, as we've pointed out, is called "structured programming," which involves starting your Adventure program (or any computer program) "from the top down," working the main components of the program out in broad strokes before fleshing it out with details. This means that there is an overall structure to the program which is not obscured by the actual code.

The Adventures in this book were all written *after* an outline for the structure was developed. In essence, the programs consist of a "master loop" at the beginning of the program which calls each of the activities the program must carry out. Each of these activities is in a separate subroutine. The subroutines can be developed, and debugged, one by one. If an error is found, for example, in the way the contents of a room are printed out, it is far easier to go straight to a routine headed "ROOM CONTENTS" than it would be to wade through 20K of program.

Of course, in the real world, things are rarely as neat as they are in theory, and my programs are not as clean and transparent as I might have hoped. Reworking areas of code tends to muddy the work of even the best-intentioned programmer. In the ideal world, an Adventure program might start like this:

```
 10  REM NAME OF ADVENTURE
 20  GOSUB 9000:REM INITIALIZE
 30  GOSUB 8000:REM PRINT PLAYER ATTRIBUTE
 40  GOSUB 1000:REM PRINT ROOM DESCRIPTION
 50  GOSUB 8000:REM CHECK IF MONSTER PRESENT,
                AND IF SO, PRINT DESCRIPTION
 60  GOSUB 7000:REM CHECK IF TREASURE
                PRESENT, AND IF SO, PRINT
                DESCRIPTION
 70  GOSUB 2000:REM ACCEPT PLAYER INPUT
 80  IF player wants to pick something up then GOSUB 2500
 90  IF player wants to fight then GOSUB
     3000. . . . . . . . . and so on
150  GOTO 30
```

A structure similar to this was written for each of the programs in this book, before I really had much idea how I was to accomplish the goals I had set myself in any of the subroutines.

All programs were written out completely on paper before the computer was even turned on, so that the game could be "hand run" before starting to grapple with it on the computer. This made it possible to catch the worst bugs right at the beginning.

I strongly advise you to follow a similar process when you write programs. I had read this advice myself, in several articles and books, and—predictably enough—had ignored it, until I found myself on a two week holiday without a computer, miles from the nearest computer dealer, and with a burning desire to write a major program I had thought up.

I ended up writing most of the program out on paper. Among the many great advantages I discovered about programming in this way was the willingness with which I completely discarded whole blocks of code if they turned out to be unworkable. It is much more difficult to decide to erase a whole section of code from a program once you actually have it in the computer than it is to just tear up a piece of paper. The temptation—when the program is already in the computer—is to fiddle with it, in an attempt to make it work, at least after a fashion.

Working on paper, then, tends to prevent code which really should not be in a program from somehow being patched together to make it work.

As well as helping in the early "get it working" stage, a structured program tends to invite improvements. Once you have your first original Adventure program up and running, you can go back to it some time in the future to try and make the fight sequence more interesting, for example, by going to that part of the code which covers the Big Clash. You will not have to wade through vast acres of codes, trying to work out just what each line does, and which particular lines control the monster interaction.

These methods were used for all four programs in this book. It may prove instructive to follow through the listing of some of the programs and work out which section does what. In many programs, you'll see that I've included lines of asterisks as a REM statement. These break the program into separate modules which should help you follow the program through.

Once you have your program up and running satisfactorily, so the player can move around the environment in accord with your map, and the mechanics of "pick up," "drop," "eat," "trigger magic spell," and the rest are working, you can then start elaborating your masterpiece. The remainder of this final chapter is devoted to ideas which you can include as embroidery on your basic program.

The Purpose

There must be some reason for the player to be taking part in the Adventure. Write a brief scenario explaining where and why the Adventure is taking place. Give the player a realistic goal (such as to survive till he or she escapes, as in our Adventures), or to find the Golden

Horn of Apostraphe and bring it safely back to base, to beat the Monster Hunting Club of America's current record of 342 of the beasties bagged in one session, to rescue the prince stranded at the top of his Castle Tower, or whatever. Make the purpose clear to the player, and make sure a significant percentage of the acts he or she takes part in are related to the achievement of the goal.

The Player Character

Instead of allowing the computer's random number generator to produce the initial character (with x points of intelligence and y of brute strength and only z of magic power), you could perhaps provide for the player to build his or her character from scratch, and then set it out on the Adventure. Running through the same Adventure a number of times with different characters could be very interesting. Of course, you'd have to put limits on the attributes a character could acquire, or you'd have some greedy soul taking the next ten million games worth of strength to be totally beyond defeat. He or she could just blunder wholesale through the environment, crushing all comers.

Experience

You may well wish to provide an opportunity to save a program while it is underway, so a player would not be forced to abort a complex Adventure in mid-flight and then retrace his or her early steps in order to try and solve it. The player's "experience" (attributes, cash, weapons, and the like) would also be saved along with the game in progress.

Quartermastering

Don't settle for just swords and broad axes. Use your imagination to offer a player a host of goodies. Rope often comes in useful. Let a player pass an apparently worthless coil of rope in one room, when six rooms later it is needed to get down a cliff (in the same way the silver key is needed for the first locked door in Citadel) and a player will soon learn that not only weapons and booty should be carried.

Magic

In "real life" role-playing games, combat and magic use are two of the highlights. Because of the infinite variety of magic spells which could be imagined (from causing the ground to fall open beneath an enemy's feet to turning into a canary and singing until everyone goes crazy) it is extremely difficult to program your computer to respond to magic in the same flexible way a Dungeon Master may do. However, we have seen two types of magic in our games (instant, random teleportation and battle victory) and there is no reason at all why you should not add as many additional kinds of magic as you like. Perhaps you might allow your player to choose from a menu of spells at the start of a game, before he or she knew what sort of problems lay ahead. They could have specific effects, which you could spell out in the program, or in notes provided for the player.

Limits

Assign a weight to each object which the player can find, and let the player know that he or she has only limited strength. Soon, the player will have to determine whether it is better to shuck the chain mail armor in order to carry a brace of invisibility spells, or to stick with the hardware and hope the wizardware won't be needed.

Research

Get a few popular history books. Early battle descriptions will give you a host of ideas to convert into terrain, weaponry, enemy reactions, and so on. Every period you read about will suggest at least one Adventure and probably more. The time and place will do much of the work involved in creating the background to the environment.

Handy Extras

As well as offering the player goodies throughout the environment (such as the map we mentioned), you could start with a much bigger arsenal than we have in the programs in this book. How about a small group of mercenaries, who can be sacrificed as dragon fodder, or a pack pony to carry your loot?

Alternative Treks

If one of the purposes of the Adventure campaign is to amass as much treasure as possible, you might like to allow for the player to backtrack from time to time to dump his or her treasure in safety at the entrance, before moving back into the dungeon or whatever. A group of bandits, hidden in room 34, will probably take everything our hapless player is carrying, so if some valuables have already been spirited away—out of the main theater of war—all is not lost.

Time Limits

If you feel some of your Adventures are a little too simple to solve, enhance them by including a real time clock in the program, one which counts down on the screen. This will keep the pressure up, and adds another layer of interest.

Climate

You might like to introduce elements of weather into your environment. A very cold room which means the player must burn something from his or her supplies to survive is one possibility. Another room could be filled with steam, which rusts swords but leaves axes untouched. A slimy floor can produce its own complications. You are sure to be able to think of other climate-like environmental factors which will help maintain interest.

There are a number of other ideas you might like to incorporate into your Adventures, such as the following:

- A monster which does not stay passively in one room, but follows you relentlessly, once you've woken him up.
- A few other "pseudo-players" under the computer's control which appear to be exploring the environment as well. The player can meet these people from time to time, possibly getting information about future dangers from them.
- A "help" command for the player to invoke if he or she feels hopelessly lost. A severe penalty (such as half the player's gold) should be extracted for using this option to ensure it is not used frequently.
- Doors can be locked, impassable, stuck, or traps. Walls can fall in on players, floors give way to a gaping crevasse, and so on. Pictures can slide from walls, hitting our hapless player on the head, and so on. You might like to create an environment just for paranoid players, where every element seems hell-bent on injury.

And so on. I'm sure by now you've got a hundred ideas in your head just waiting to be expressed as Adventure programs. Good Adventuring. The suggestions for further reading in the appendix may well serve as sources of other ideas to incorporate into your own Adventures.

May the Dreaded Ice-Dragon not molest you, and may all your chests be filled with Elven Gold.

APPENDICES

1 Suggestions for Further Reading

There is an impressive body of support literature for Adventure gaming, as a visit to your local Games shop will demonstrate. The selection which follows is very much a product of my own interest in the field, and it should not be seen as even an attempt at selecting the "best" publications. However, the list is made up from those works which I've found of interest and value. There are probably over a hundred of equal worth, but at least this list should give you a starting point:

THROUGH DUNGEONS DEEP: A Fantasy Gamers' Handbook—Robert Plamondon (Reston Publishing Company, Inc., Reston, Virginia, 1982)

What is Dungeons and Dragons®—John Butterfield, Philip Parker and David Honigmann (Penguin Books Ltd., Harmondsworth, Middlesex, England, 1982) [*Dungeons and Dragons* is the adventure game which was originated by TSR Hobbies Inc.™ The term is a registered trademark.]

Dicing with Dragons, an Introduction to Role-Playing Games—Ian Livingstone (Routledge & Kegan Paul, London, Melbourne and Henley, 1982)

Fantasy Role-Playing Games—J. Eric Holmes (Hippocrene Books, Inc., New York, 1981)

As well as books, there are a number of game-playing aids which will help you in building the framework environment within which your Adventure will be enacted. Another good source of ideas is rule books for specific games. Among those which may help you are:

MONSTER AND TREASURE ASSORTMENT—TSR Games, POB 756, Lake Geneva, WI 53147, 1980, distributed by Random House, Inc. This publication, which comes in a variety of "sets" and "levels" is a great place for getting ideas for monster names and treasure descriptions.

DUNGEON GEOMORPHS—Also produced by TSR Games, the "geomorphs" are a number of rectangular and square map sections, which can be fitted together in an infinite variety of ways to form dungeon and cavern floor plans.

BOOK 0, AN INTRODUCTION TO TRAVELLER—Loren K. Wiseman (Games Designers' Workshop Inc., POB 1646, Bloomington, IL 61701). This is an example of the rule book I mentioned. *Traveller* is a science-fiction Adventure in the far future, and BOOK 0 is an introduction to the concepts of role-playing with specific attention to Traveller. As Book 0 points out, the "total amount of *Traveller* material available is staggering and growing all the time" (p. 11). Despite this, BOOK 0, BOOK 1, BOOK 2, and BOOK 3 are all you really need to play the game, and BOOK 0 is enough, by itself, to give you a taste for laying out Adventure programs in deepest space. Leaf through a copy at your Games shop, and you'll see how many great ideas it contains which you can apply to your own programs. Note that Traveller is a registered trademark.

DUNGEONS & DRAGONS® boxed game sets are a good way to learn some of the possibilities of Adventure gaming. You can start (and stay, if you like) with the BASIC SET WITH INTRODUCTORY MODULE. This set typically contains two books, and a set of six dice, with various numbers of sides. The books are BASIC RULES, which set out the concepts of role-playing, and explain how characters are "rolled up," how their personalities are derived, how fights are sorted out, and many aspects of the Dungeon or Game Master's role.

As well as dice and BASIC RULES, the set contains a campaign background, THE KEEP ON THE BORDERLANDS. This comes with a great deal of information, including a series of maps, room and player information, and further details on fight resolution. I feel that the BASIC RULES boxed set is probably the best source of ideas you can get your hands on. It is also a very good way to achieve greater understanding of how role-playing games are developed and controlled.

WARNING: These sources of ideas are suggested, of course, only for your own use, to produce games for your own entertainment. You cannot incorporate copyright material into programs for public sale.

2 Random Place/Monster Names

I set my computer the relatively simple task of generating names for monsters. Here's the program I used:

```
10 REM CHARACTER NAME GENERATOR
20 RANDOMIZE VAL(RIGHT$(TIME$,2))
30 DIM Z(5)
40 FOR T= 1 TO 5:READ Z(T):NEXT
50 FOR H = 1 TO 4
60 FOR T = 1 TO 4 + INT(RND(1)*4)
70 B = 0
80 A = 66 + INT(RND(1)*25)
90 IF RND(1)>.7 AND (A=69 OR A = 73 OR A
 = 79 OR A = 85) THEN 80
100 IF (T = 2 OR T = 5 OR T=7) THEN B= Z
(INT(RND(1)*5))
110 IF B<>0 THEN LPRINT CHR$(B);:GOTO 13
0
120 LPRINT CHR$(A);
130 NEXT T
140 LPRINT "    ";
150 NEXT H
160 LPRINT
170 GOTO 50
180 DATA 65,69,73,79,85
```

And here are some (I got rid of the hopeless ones) of the results of running it, producing a number of names you might like to incorporate into your programs either as names of monsters or as mythical place names:

```
LAQH      REBLEP    IAMD     TIGNEZA
QOUHEXE   PISBI     OAKHO    BIHLA
GEDIE     CISWAH    VELN     NEYH
GOJUO     PAWTOZI   NAOJM    MEDSA
```

TEHOOVO	GAMLO	BEDO	HEZRI
MEZPO	KISC	MANMY	KOMNOMO
JELM	LESH	YXPHI	VEDLE
EANBENG	YIQC	DOXT	FATGEKA
BEZMAZI	LIIYEX	NIGRAP	HOPNOG
COLOAZ	SALUENI	NEYOKEE	LOBIEBE
POGWOR	ROKVA	POYNOZ	GODWUR
XEZKE	JEBJO	NEYMEO	WOOF
RECCI	XEVFI	MIDO	MATWEO
GOUL	KEBGA	CEXFAV	JEXV
ZAHNIL	OIYYI	FEBSEX	ZONHIP
JAPDANZ	QINNAYP	VEBXOI	LOCQI
POBLIP	GOLJEB	IERVO	COER
CIKWAB	TEEQAFO	ZARW	FAHSEYA
HOKM	DIRI	GEXNAC	HEHKO
XOEOPU	BIRWAI	YEQMIIE	SAFWOLI
FIDWIY	PAWK	DAHI	COJJOLA
VINPERO	XITFO	JEMR	MOXKO
TEYLENO	LERE	DOQKII	VOCVOF
ZIZS	PAFXI	YOXLO	NISL
RAJYOR	WACNA	YALDAR	BIDBIF
POLVO	LYMC	TERC	WAFMOK
XENTADN	REZN	WILTEG	DINWOL
GEYP	CINQOCA	QABYI	WOKIA

3 Useful Addresses

Adventure Games Manufacturers, USA:

Adventure Games Inc., 871 Edgerton St., St. Paul, MN 55101

Attack Wargaming Association, 314 Edgley Ave., Glenside, PA 19038

Avalon Hill, 4517 Harford Road, Baltimore, MD 21214

Chaosium Inc., POB 6302, Albany, CA 94706

Command Perspectives, 3522 Polk Avenue, San Diego, CA 92104

Creative Wargamers Workshop, Inc., 330 East 6th Street, Suite 1E, New York, NY 10003

Excalibre Games, POB 29171, Brooklyn Center, MN 55429

Fantasy Games Unlimited, Inc., POB 182, Roslyn, NY 11576

Flying Buffalo Inc., POB 1467, Scottsdale, AZ 82852

Game Designers' Workshop, 203 North St., Normal, IL 61761

Gamescience, 10956 Pass Road, Gulfport, MA 39501

Grimoire Games, POB 4363, Berkeley, CA 94704

Heritage USA, POB 345125, Dallas, TX 75234

Hero Games, 425 Harbor Boulevard, Belmont, CA 94002

Imperium Publishing Co., POB 9854, Minneapolis, MN 55440

Infocom, Inc., 55 Wheeler St., Cambridge, MA 02138

Judges Guild (Task Force Games), 1165 N University, Decatur, IL 62526

Metagaming Concepts, POB 15346, Austin, TX 78761

Simulations Publications, Inc., 257 Park Avenue South, New York, NY 10010

TRS Hobbies, POB 110, Lake Geneva, WI 53147

Magazines

Adventure Gaming, Manzaak Publishing, Inc., POB 12291, Norwood, OH 45212

Alarums and Excursions, 396 South Alla Road, Los Angeles, CA 90060

Ares, Simulations Publications, Inc., 257 Park Avenue South, New York, NY 10010

The Dragon, TRS Periodicals, Inc., POB 110, Lake Geneva, WI 53147

Different Worlds, Chaosium, Inc., POB 6302, Albany, CA 94706

High Passage, FASA, POB 6930, Chicago, IL 60680

Interplay, Metagaming, POB 15346, Austin, TX 78761

The Journal of the Travellers' Aid Society, POB 432, Normal, IL 61761

The Judges Guild Journal/The Dungeoneer/Pegasus, Judges Guild, 1165 North University Ave., Decatur, IL 62526

Nexus, Task Force Games, 1110 North Fillmore, Amarillo, TX 79107

Sorcerer's Apprentice, Flying Buffalo, Inc., POB 1467, Scottsdale, AZ 85252

The Space Gamer, POB 18805, Austin, TX 78760

The Wild Hunt, 71 Beacon St., Arlington, MA 02174